P9-DEB-237

MAKING GLORIOUS
GIFTS
FROM YOUR GARDEN

MAKING GLORIOUS
GIFTS
FROM YOUR GARDEN

By Marie Browning

Sterling Publishing Co., Inc.
New York

PROLIFIC IMPRESSIONS
PRODUCTION STAFF:

Editor: Mickey Baskett
Copy: Phyllis Mueller
Graphics: Dianne Miller, Prepress XPress
Photography: Frances Litman, Victoria, BC
Administration: Jim Baskett

Every effort has been made to insure that the information presented is accurate. Since we have no control over physical conditions, individual skills, or chosen tools and products, the publisher disclaims any liability for injuries, losses, untoward results, or any other damages which may result from the use of the information in this book. Thoroughly read the instructions for all products used to complete the projects in this book, paying particular attention to all cautions and warnings shown for that product to ensure their proper and safe use.

No part of this book may be reproduced for commercial purposes in any form without permission by the copyright holder. The written instructions and design patterns in this book are intended for the personal use of the reader and may be reproduced for that purpose only.

Library of Congress Cataloging-in-Publication Data Available

10 9 8 7 6 5 4 3 2

First paperback edition published in 2000 by
Sterling Publishing Company, Inc.
387 Park Avenue South, New York, N.Y. 10016
© 1999 by Prolific Impressions, Inc.
Distributed in Canada by Sterling Publishing
℅ Canadian Manda Group, One Atlantic Avenue, Suite 105
Toronto, Ontario, Canada M6K 3E7
Distributed in Great Britain and Europe by Cassell PLC
Wellington House, 125 Strand, London WC2R 0BB, England
Distributed in Australia by Capricorn Link (Australia) Pty Ltd.
P.O. Box 6651, Baulkham Hills, Business Centre, NSW 2153, Australia

Printed in China
All rights reserved

Sterling ISBN 0-8069-2479-9 Trade
            0-8069-2515-9 Paper

ABOUT THE AUTHOR
Marie Browning

Marie Browning is a consummate craft designer, making a career of designing products, writing books and articles, plus teaching and demonstrating. You may have already been charmed by her creative designs and not even been aware; as she has designed stencils, stamps, transfers, and a vareity of other products for national art & craft supply companies.

You may also have enjoyed books and articles by Marie. She is the author of two other books published by Sterling, *Natural Soapmaking* (1998) and *Handcrafted Journals, Albums, Scrapbooks, & More* (1999). Her articles and designs have appeared in *Handcraft Illustrated, Better Homes & Gardens, Canadian Stamper, Great American Crafts, All American Crafts*, and in numerous project books published by Plaid Enterprises, Inc.

Browning earned a Fine Arts Diploma from Camosun College and attended the University of Victoria. She is a Certified Professional Demonstrator, a professional affiliate of the Canadian Craft and Hobby Association, and a member of the Stencil Artisan's League and the Society of Craft Designers.

Marie Browning lives, gardens, and crafts on Vancouver Island in Canada. She and her husband Scott have three children: Katelyn, Lena, and Jonathan. ∾

Acknowledgements

I owe an infinite bouquet to the many people who have given me the unconditional encouragement, time, gardening and culinary talents, and friendship that made creating this book a wonderful experience that I will treasure.

For the beautiful photography, Frances Litman. It was a joy to work with such a talented, fun, and professional artist. I hope this is a beginning.

Tremendous thanks to my editor, Mickey Baskett, who believed in my suggestions. You took a chance, and I am deeply appreciative.

Many friends lent a helping hand, providing props and accessories: Jan from the Folk Art Connection, Karen Evans, Corrine and John Kempling for the beautiful roses, Sharon Vermaning, Muriel Canton, and Joyce Meline. Many, many thanks to Julie from House Dressing—the supplies truly made the difference in creating the beautiful images in the book.

*After many days of fun and hard work, the ladies have bonded. **(left to right)**: Marie Browning (author), Frances Litman (photographer), Mickey Baskett (editor)*

The most wonderful thing about having a large family is that they are always there to help. Mom and Dad, you gave me so much, from a day from your busy schedule to help tidy my garden to the loan of your plants. Mom B., your advice was always right on. I thank my wonderful sisters, Cathy and Sharon, for their talents and the rest of the gang—Teresa, Bill, Jamie, and Lisa, and their families for their enthusiasm. A note of thanks to Uncle Bud, Aunt Liz, Uncle Mike, Aunt Julie, Aunt Joselyn, Uncle Barney, and Adele for your gardening wisdom and the extra color. An extra special thanks to Uncle Tom for all the wonderful gardening antiques and props—the support, encouragement, and love you give to me with all my ventures means a great deal. Your belief in me and your love and support makes the task so much easier, from the prayers from Father Joe to just being there.

Finally, to my wonderful husband Scott and my children—Katelyn, Lena, and Jonathan—you put up with so much, from taste tasting recipes to the dried flowers in the family room—my love and gratefulness.

Marie Browning

CONTENTS

Pressed Flower Pretties

The delicacy of pressed petals can create enchanting greeting cards, coasters, sachets, decorated soaps, and more.

Dried Flower Decorations

Dry your flowers and herbs and use them in arrangements, to decorate baskets, to make garlands, and more.

Twig & Vine Projects

Nothing need go to waste in the garden--even the twigs can be used to make easels and decorate frames, while vines can be easily woven into wreaths.

Packaging Like a Pro

Tips and techniques for packaging and presenting your harvest as gifts.

Theme Gift Baskets

Ideas for combining a variety of items to create special gift baskets for all occasions.

Index

Metric Conversion

A HARVEST OF GARDEN-INSPIRED GIFTS, THEME BASKETS, AND PACKAGING IDEAS

*I*n this hectic, commercially driven world, making gifts from the preserved bounty of your garden is a way to be transported back to an amiable, domestic time when most gifts were homemade, one-of-a-kind treasures. You also give one of the most valuable gifts today—the gift of your time.

I don't claim to be a gardening expert; rather, I am a crafter who loves to garden. I like plants that are useful as well as attractive, and I am always looking for new ones to use in my creative endeavors. My inspiration comes from many sources. I am lucky to live in a garden paradise that boasts a Zone 9 climate and mild winters. My village is located minutes from Victoria on Vancouver Island in Canada. Just down the street are the world famous Butchart Gardens, and I am surrounded by expert gardeners and nurseries at every corner.

I used a variety of plant materials in creating products for this book, focusing on easily grown herbs. These wonderful, useful, and aromatic plants can be cultivated anywhere. They will grow happily in containers on an apartment balcony, in a large country garden, or on a porch in the suburbs. Even if you don't have a garden, you can visit a farmer's market and purchase flowers, fresh herbs, and vegetables to create your offerings.

I also have found many ideas and recipes from turn of the century cookbooks, household guides, and "Girl's Own" annuals. My favorite is *Smiley's Cookbook and Universal Household Guide* published in 1894. I am motivated by the extent of knowledge housekeepers possessed at that time, when everything was made from scratch. It is fun to adapt old recipes to modern kitchens and ingredients.

This book shows you how to preserve your harvest and introduces techniques for creating home and personal fragrance gifts and culinary treats. You'll also see how to package the gifts professionally and attractively, both individually and as theme baskets.

Enjoy growing, harvesting, preserving, creating, and—most of all—giving.

Marie Browning

FAVORITE PLANTS & HERBS

A garden reflects the gardener, and my garden is a reflection of my crafting passion. Most plants in my garden can be used to create craft projects, for home or personal fragrance crafting, or to decorate my home. They provide color, scent, and interest. The plants you choose to grow in your garden will reflect your personal interests and tastes and the climate where you live.

The most useful plant for home and personal fragrance crafting and culinary crafting is the herb. Herbs are also the easiest plants to grow. The American Herb Society's official definition is "any plant that can be used for pleasure, fragrance, or physic," which makes for a very lengthy list! Check with local garden societies or consult garden guides published for your area to determine the best plant varieties for you.

No matter what plants you grow in your garden, you will be able to use the preserving methods in this book to share the bounty with others.

My Favorites

These are my all time favorite plants to grow for fragrance, cooking, and general crafting. These plants grow well in my area and have been successful for me. All parts of plants are used; petals, leaves, seeds, barks, roots, berries, and fruit. Most are very easy to grow.

- **Roses** *(Rosa)* The rose scent is the most popular and irresistible of all floral scents, and the rose has been the symbol of love for centuries. All types of roses are useful to grow. The old fashioned types are more fragrant and have lots of petals for potpourri—look for roses labeled "damascena" for the strongest scents. Modern roses dry well by hanging as well as in silica gel. Climbing and miniature roses make wonderful dried rosebuds and are excellent when preserved with sugar.

- **Scented Geraniums** *(Pelargonium)* Scented geraniums are grown for their highly scented leaves, not for flowers. Scented geraniums are useful in potpourri, sachets, personal fragrance crafting, and culinary crafting. There are many varieties and fragrances from which to choose—one mail-order garden center lists 80 different types! My favorites are the rose, peppermint, and fruit scented varieties. Some I buy just because I love the thought of growing "pink champagne" or "chocolate mint." They are a joy to brush up against in the garden when they release their beautiful fresh aromas. The peppermint scented geranium has large, fuzzy leaves that children love to "pet." Scented geraniums are easily dried by hanging or pressing.

- **Lemon Verbena** *(Aloysia triphylla)* This plant has a gorgeous floral-lemon scent in both the leaves and the small white flowers. The long pointed leaves are very aromatic and air dry well for potpourri and sachets. Lemon verbena does very well when planted in a container that can be moved during the winter months—the tender shrub will die if not protected from temperatures below 15 degrees F.

- **Lavender** *(Lavandula)* A popular and well known traditional herb, lavender has spikes of highly fragrant purple, pink, or white buds on strong stems. Lavender has been used in fragrant baths and perfumed beauty products for centuries. Its name lavender comes from the Latin *lavare,* which means "to wash." Dry growing conditions yield the maximum oils. Harvest the buds just before full bloom and hang to dry.

- **Mint** *(Mentha)* This refreshing herb has many varieties. Orange bergamot is best for potpourri; apple mint is my favorite for culinary crafting. These prolific plants will grow in any shady area of your garden and can become invasive if not controlled. The leaves can be air dried by hanging or pressed, candied, or preserved in vinegar. The scent is cooling and refreshing, and the plant's antiseptic properties cleanses the air as it dries.

- **Hydrangea** *(Hydrangea macrophylla)* These large mop-head flower clusters are beautiful in dried arrangements and the individual flowers are my all-time favorite flower for pressing. Hydrangea grows very well in my area, and I take full advantage of the many colors and varieties available. A favorite is the *Hydrangea paniculata grandiflora,* often called "pee gee hydrangea," which has spectacular white blooms.

- **Rosemary** *(Rosmarinus officinalis)* Rosemary is an easy to grow evergreen herb that has a distinctive scent and is a popular culinary herb and landscape plant. It is valuable for fragrance crafting in simmers and potpourri and is a useful herb for sleep sachets. A symbol of remembrance and fidelity, rosemary is used in wedding bouquets. Rosemary can easily be trained into topiaries and bonsai and can be harvested and preserved any time for its precious and useful oils. ∽

Favorite plants: Miniature pink rose, pee gee hydrangea, rose scented geranium, lavender 'Grosso', apple mint, and a rosemary topiary.

Gathering from the Wild

Please remember to preserve nature and obey local ordinances. In many areas, there are stiff fines for removing plants, cutting branches, or even gathering pine cones on public lands. Never completely strip a plant of flowers, leaves, berries, or seeds—you might be taking an animal's food supply. On private property, be sure to have the owner's permission to collect botanicals. If land is being cleared for construction, it may be possible to obtain permission to gather plants and mosses. Be very careful not to disturb the fragile ecosystems of national and local parks so their beauty can be enjoyed for generations. ∾

Lemon verbena.

PRESERVING THE HARVEST

The following pages show you practical methods for preserving your plant materials. Learning to preserve plants extends the beauty of your garden beyond the growing season and allows you to share its bounty.

Air Drying

Air drying is the easiest and most effective method for drying herbs and flowers. Purchased dried materials will never be as good as the freshly dried botanicals you can create yourself. Your colors will be brighter, the specimens will not be crushed from transporting, and because the plants are fresher, the aromas and flavors will be more intense. By not using pesticides or herbicides in your garden, you also will have complete control over the purity and cleanliness of your plants.

The best dried plants come from the best fresh specimens. You will be disappointed if you choose plants for drying that are past their prime or have insect or disease damage. Most flowers are best just before full bloom. Choose a sunny day for cutting, after the morning dew has evaporated and before the full heat of the noonday sun. Arm yourself with a basket, sharp cutting shears, and paper and a pen to record plant types. Choose the best technique for drying your harvested plant by the way you are going to use it. For example, rose petals for potpourri should be strewn in a low box or on a screen, while rose heads for flower arranging should hang to dry.

Your drying location should be a dark, dry room with good air circulation and (preferably) a high ceiling. Darkness is important so the colors do not fade. Placing the specimens in a closed closet or stuffy room invites mold and mildew to settle on your harvest. A laundry room is usually not a good choice because of the excess moisture from the washing and drying of clothes. If you live in an area where the humidity is high, special care must be taken in drying the specimens. You may need to "jump start" the drying process with a microwave oven or use a dehydrator to ensure success.

The moisture content of most plants is quite high—they contain up to 70% water. The aim is to dry the specimens quickly but retain the essential oils. You will be surprised to see how much the plant material will shrink (a box full of fresh rose petals makes only a few cups of dried petals). The colors also intensify; dark red roses dry to a black color, and light pink roses dry to a dark pink.

The drying times of different flowers vary greatly. Lavender, with very little moisture, takes only a week to fully dry. A rose, which has a lot more moisture, can take up to three weeks. The area where you're drying and the weather—especially the humidity—outside also are factors.

Proper storage is important for successful projects. The specimens must be completely dry, with no hint of dampness. If the petals and leaves have just a little moisture left in them, they will mold and turn brown. It's better to be safe. A dry, dark location with even temperature is best for storing. I like to wrap dried botanicals on the stem loosely in tissue paper, then place them in a large basket. Petals and dried leaves can be stored successfully in a clean, airtight container in a dry, dark place. I do not highly recommend plastic to store your dried botanicals, but sometimes it is the most economical and practical storage container. Never leave the container on a sunny window ledge—the condensation will cause the botanicals to mold and turn brown. Remember to label each botanical with the name, harvest date, and storage date. Use your harvest within a year to ensure freshness and optimum fragrance. ∽

Air Drying

▓ Air Drying with Screens

It's best to dry botanicals on a screen when you wish individual petals for potpourri and simmers or if the specimen's stem is too short for hanging. For example, if you hang dry rose heads and then take them apart for individual petals, you will be disappointed because the petals in the middle of the flower will be brown. However, if you remove the petals from the rose head when fresh and dry the petals in a single layer on a screen, you will be rewarded with perfectly dried petals, with no browning. Short stemmed herbs such as thyme and sweet woodruff are a bit bulky to hang dry, so drying on screens is preferable. Grasses, mosses, seed pods, and cones are also suitable for screen drying.

You Will Need:

Flowers and/or leafy herbs

Wooden frames with wire mesh screens OR cardboard boxes with the sides cut down to a height of 3-4". (The cardboard trays that hold canned drinks are excellent for drying.) **Never** use a soiled box or one with a wax or plastic coating.

Here's How:

1. Remove the petals from the flower heads and lay on the screen in a single layer. (I do this outside while I gather the petals to give any critters time to escape.) I prefer to keep colors separate, even if it means taking up a large screen for only a few flower heads of petals.
2. Stack the screens or boxes for even air flow.
3. Shake and toss the petals every day to help them dry on all sides. **Never** add fresh petals to partially dried petals—you will re-introduce moisture and your specimens could turn brown.
4. As the petals or leaves dry, they will shrink considerably. You may want a series of smaller screens or boxes to finish the drying process to free up the larger screens and boxes for a fresh batch. ∽

▓ "Jump Starting" with a Microwave

Some botanicals benefit from first drying in a microwave oven. Parsley and basil tend to keep their bright green color—they don't turn brown like they do when air dried. You may want to try this technique with flower petals if you live in an area with high humidity.

You Will Need:

Leaves on stems   A microwave oven
Paper towels

Here's How:

1. Remove the leaves from the stems.
2. Place approximately 1 cup leaves on a paper towel in the microwave. Microwave on high for one minute.
3. Remove from the oven and let cool before transferring to a screen to complete drying. The leaves will still be limp and moist, but the drying process will have had a head start. Do not be tempted to over microwave. Overheating will damage the essential oils and your dried botanicals will not have a strong fragrance or flavor. ∽

▓ Drying Pine Cones

Some pine cones are sticky when gathered with a little pitch on them; others may not have opened. I like to bake cones in the oven to remove the excess pitch and let them dry out and fully open. Oven drying also kills any insects that may still be in the cones. Baking moss, bark, and twigs in an oven is useful for killing any eggs or larvae that could otherwise hatch in your home.

Here's How:

Line a large baking pan with foil. Fill with pine cones. Bake in a 250 degree F. oven for 1/2 to 1 hour, or until the cones are fully opened. The fresh pine aroma that fills your home while you bake the cones is a wonderful bonus.

Wiring Pine Cones for Arrangements:
Use 22 gauge stem wire to wire pine cones.

GOOD PLANTS FOR DRYING ON SCREENS

Birch bark
Cones and seed pods
Grasses (wheat, bamboo, rush)
Lichens
Peony petals
Poppy petals
Rosebuds (small ones)
Rose petals
Short stemmed herbs (sweet woodruff, thyme)
Strawflowers
Sunflower petals
Twigs and branches

GOOD PLANTS FOR DRYING UPRIGHT IN A VASE

Shasta daisies
Grasses
Poppy seed heads

Petals air drying on wire mesh screens.

Drying Pine Cones (cont.)

Push one end of the wire around the lowest band of scales and twist the ends tightly to hold. With needle nose pliers, hold the ends of the wire while twisting the pine cone to move the wire close to the inside of the cone and invisible. If wiring small pine cones, use a finer gauge wire. Cover the exposed wire with brown florist's tape to create a natural looking stem. The wired cones can be taped together with florist's tape to form long branches. As a guide, study how pine cones grow on branches. ∽

▪ Air Drying Flowers by Hanging

You Will Need:

Flowers
Rubber bands
Wire coat hangers
Sharp shears
Labels for recording botanical name and harvest date

Here's How:

1. Cut the flowers when the dew is dried and the flowers are open. (Flowers are at their peak just after they open.) Harvest leaves just before the flowers open for the maximum oil content.
2. Strip off the leaves at the bottom of the stem where the bunch will be bound to increase the strength of the stems and speed up drying. Stems with many leaves become too brittle when dried, so leave on just a few.
3. Gather up a small bunch, making sure they have sufficient air circulation (they shouldn't be too bunched up), and secure with a rubber band.
4. Holding the bunch by the stem ends, slip the rubber band over the bottom of the coat hanger and secure the bunched stems. This method is quick and holds the bunch as it dries. If you use string or raffia to bind botanicals for drying, your flowers and leaves will end up all over the floor because the stems shrink as they dry. A rubber band holds the bunch tight during the whole drying process.
5. Slip a paper label on each hanger for identification.
6. Hang your completed hangers in a dark, dry, well ventilated room away from direct sunlight. ∽

▪ Wiring Flower Stems for Hang Drying

If a flower's stem is damaged, short, or weak, cut the flower head off the stem and insert a wire stem. Flowers that benefit from having wire stems include strawflowers, roses, asters, and dahlias.

You Will Need:

Flowers
Wire cutters
22 gauge wire
Sharp shears

Here's How:

1. Remove the flower head from the stem with the shears.
2. Cut a 10" piece of wire and make a small hook at one end.
3. Push the straight end of the wire through the center of the flower head and pull the hook down into the center of the flower.
4. Hang to dry. As the flower dries, the calyx will shrink around the wire and hold it tight. Blossoms must be wired while the flower is fresh, otherwise the calyx dries rock hard and the wire cannot pass through it. To avoid having the wire showing when arranging, slip the wire stem into a hollow stem from a larkspur or shasta daisy to cover the wire and make a natural stem. ∽

▪ Drying Hydrangeas

Harvest hydrangeas after the mini flower in the center of each flower has bloomed and the petals feel papery.

Hang drying: Weave the hydrangea stems through vertically mounted chicken wire mesh. (Other heavy headed specimens also work well with this method, including artichokes, sunflowers, thistles, and onion seed heads.)

Water drying: Place freshly cut flowers with long stems in a large vase with about 3" of water. Place in a warm, dark area. Let the flowers slowly absorb the water and dry naturally in the vase. Other plants that do well with this method include onion seed heads, sea lavender, baby's breath, and bulrushes. ∽

GOOD PLANTS FOR HANG DRYING

Artemisia
Asters
Carnations
Cornflower
Dahlias
Delphinium
Globe amaranth
Gypsophilia (baby's breath)
Heather
Hydrangeas (see "Drying Hydrangeas")
Larkspur
Lavender
Leafy herbs
Nigella
Pearly everlasting
Peonies
Roses
Santolina
Statice
Strawflowers *
Tansy
Thistles
Yarrow

* When harvesting strawflowers, pick the blossoms when the buds just start to open. They will continue to open as they dry to form a perfect blossom.

Hang drying hydrangeas

Drying Flowers Using Desiccants

A desiccant is a drying agent that absorbs moisture. Common desiccants include silica gel, borax, cornmeal, and clean sand. Flowers dried this way keep their color, shape, and size better than they do when air dried, but the flowers are very fragile and can shatter easily. Finished desiccant-dried flowers can be used in floral arrangements, to accent potpourri, or in other dried flower creations.

I prefer silica gel to both borax and sand. Sand is heavy and does not absorb moisture as fast as silica gel, so the flowers can end up misshapen or brown. Borax can leave a white powder on blossoms that must be carefully and painstakingly removed with a soft brush after drying.

Silica gel is a dry white crystal that can absorb up to 40% its weight in water vapor. (During manufacture, it's a gel—hence, the name.) It comes ready to use with color indicator crystals that are blue when the silica gel is dry and turn white or pink when the moisture limit has been absorbed. When the crystals turn pink, simply place the silica gel in a foil lined pan and bake in a 250 degree oven for 1 hour or until the crystals turn blue again. Silica gel is expensive to buy, but the crystals can be used over and over again for preserving perfect flower heads. As the crystals will absorb moisture from the air, store silica gel in an airtight tin or plastic container with a tight-fitting lid.

CAUTION: Silica gel should not be consumed. Take extra care when working in the kitchen, as the crystals resemble sugar. Clean up all spills immediately and keep children away. Wear a mask so you won't breathe the dust. ∾

Silica Gel Drying Method

Flowers that are three-fourths open are best dried with silica gel.

You Will Need:
Flowers
Silica gel crystals
A container with a lid deep enough to hold the flowers (I like to use a cookie tin)

Here's How:
1. Place a layer of crystals in the bottom of the container, about 1/2 to 1" deep. Cut the flower heads, leaving a short stem. *Option:* Add a wire stem, following the instructions in the Hang Drying section.
2. Arrange the flower heads in the silica gel, making sure none are touching. If the flowers are wired, bend the wire at a 45 degree angle at the point where it comes out from the flower and place into the crystals.
3. Completely cover the flowers with the crystals, spooning the crystals around the blossoms so they maintain their natural shape.
4. Place the cover on the container, seal with tape (if needed for an airtight fit), and place in a dry area. Check the flowers in two days. How long it takes will vary with the size, texture, and moisture content of the blooms. Small flowers like violets and miniature roses take two to three days, while peonies and large roses take four to five days.
5. To remove the flowers, carefully pour off the silica gel until the flowers are uncovered. Lift the flowers out gently and blow away any particles that have adhered to the petals. Remove any remaining silica gel with a small, soft paint brush. *Note:* Roses, carnations, and other flowers with a large calyx need additional drying time—the petals will dry, but the thick calyx will still be moist. Push the calyx into the crystals, with the petals on top, cover the container, and let dry for another day. This prevents the petals from over-drying. ∾

Silica Drying with a Microwave Oven

This method is a combination of silica gel drying and air drying that produces a flower with the color and shape of a silica dried blossom, but the strength of an air dried blossom. It's very quick and simple, but you have to take care not to over-dry the flowers or they will become brittle and break into a pile of crumbs. The best results are achieved when you use one type of flower at a time, rather than a mix. **Do not use wired flowers in the microwave.**

You Will Need:
A plastic or glass container (a cover isn't necessary)
Silica gel
Flowers with short stems
A microwave oven
A small glass

continued on next page

Spooning silica gel over flowers.

continued from page 16

Here's How:

1. Place a thin layer of silica gel into the bottom of your container.
2. Arrange the flower heads in the silica gel, making sure none are touching.
3. Add enough silica gel to bury the flowers. Make sure the flowers are completely covered.
4. Place the container into the microwave with a small glass of water. Microwave on high for one minute. Open the oven door and gently place your hand on the crystals. If they are still cool, microwave for another minute or until the crystals are warm.
5. Remove the container from the oven and place on the counter. Let cool completely.
6. Remove the flowers by gently pouring out the crystals. The flowers will not be completely dry; place them on a paper towel and let them air dry completely. ∽

FLOWERS SUITABLE FOR SILICA GEL DRYING

Anemones
Asters
Camellias
Carnations and pinks *
Cosmos
Daffodils
Dahlias (small blossoms)
Delphiniums (individual blossoms)
Freesia
Gerbera daisies
Peonies
Roses

* After silica drying, the carnation's calyx shrinks and no longer holds the petals in place. Squirting a little craft glue into the calyx helps the blossom stay together.

Flowers dried in silica gel.

Pressing Flowers & Vegetables

Pressing plants is a simple technique that results in a two-dimensional product suitable for displaying in potpourri and under glass and for mounting on cards and labels. Flowers, leaves, vegetables, whole plants, and sea plants can be pressed with remarkable results. You can purchase pressed flowers and leaves for your creative craft projects, but they are never as nice or as varied as plants that you press yourself.

You can use a purchased flower press or microwave press, construct your own press, or use a large book for pressing your plant materials. Pressing flowers and foliage takes, on average, three to four weeks.

How to Make a Plant Press

A plant press can be a decorative accent as well as a practical tool for pressing flowers and leaves you have harvested from your garden. It can also be a welcome gift. Take the extra time to decorate your press so you can display it proudly. I find if I display the press on a table, I use it more!

You Will Need:

2 basswood plaques, 8" x 10" (These plaques, available at craft stores, come in a variety of shapes and sizes, They are kiln dried, sanded, and ready to use. If you are unable to find them, use heavy plywood free of knots.)

4 flat top wooden knobs, 1"   4 bolts

4 wing nuts   4 washers

10-12 corrugated cardboard sheets, 8" x 10"

20-24 pieces smooth, absorbent paper (I prefer rice paper, available in rolls or sheets at fine art stores. Do not use paper towels—the texture of the towel will show on the plants you press.)

Drill and drill bit (choose a drill bit with a larger diameter than the diameter of the bolts)

2 C-clamps

Wood glue

Here's How:

1. Using the C-clamps, clamp the plaques, wrong sides together, and mark holes 3/4" from each corner. Drill holes through both plaques. Remove clamps.
2. If you wish to paint and decorate the top of your press, do it now.
3. Place one plaque on your work surface. Slip the bolts through the holes. Using a strong wood glue, secure the wooden knobs over the bolt ends on the bottom of the plaque. Let dry.
4. Cut the cardboard and smooth paper into 7" x 9" pieces. Trim the corners so they fit into the press.
5. Stack the cardboard and paper in the press in the following order: cardboard, 2 sheets of paper, cardboard, 2 sheets of paper, cardboard, etc. until you've used all the cardboard.
6. Place the second plaque on top and put the washers and nuts on the bolts.

Pocket Press:

A small press can be made with two small wooden plaques that are held together with two strong rubber bands. Choose a size plaque that's convenient to pop into a backpack or picnic basket. ∽

Tips for Pressing Flowers and Leaves

- Harvest plants in the morning after the dew has dried. Collect flowers in various stages of bloom, and leaves and buds of the plant.
- Press plants as soon as possible after harvesting to prevent wilting. Place the plants between the two absorbent, smooth sheets in the press.
- For flowers with bulky stamens, place the flowers between two sheets of thin polyester batting, then place between the absorbent layers. I have successfully dried daisy-like flowers and fleshy flowers such as lily of the valley this way.
- If you use a book for pressing, place two sheets of absorbent paper between the pages to protect the book.
- Different flowers take different times to dry. Check the press in about two weeks. The plants will not be harmed if you leave them in the press after they are dry, but you can damage them if they are removed before the drying process is complete.
- Store the pressed plants flat in labeled envelopes. ∽

Botanical Pressing

When botanists press specimen plants, they are careful to collect samples of the entire plant—leaves, stems, seeds, flowers, and roots. Sometimes the entire plant is uprooted and pressed. Essential information such as the name of the plant, date collected, place of collection, and notes about the habitat are recorded. Such botanical pressings make interesting specimens for cards or to keep as a journal. Wash any soil from the roots, dry the plant, and press. ∽

Microwave Pressing

Flower presses for the microwave are easy to use, and you can create pressed flowers almost instantly. I found the color

continued on next page

A full-size, homemade flower press. At lower right, a pocket press.

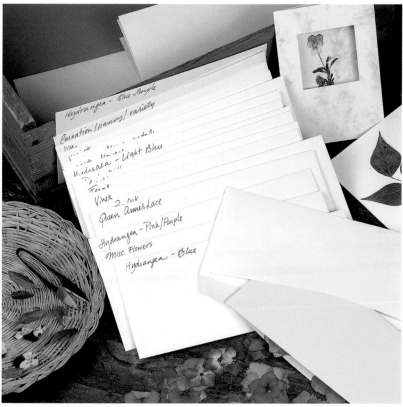

A filing system for pressed flowers.

continued from page 18

retained with the microwave press was excellent. I also was able to press thick, fleshy flowers that would be difficult to press with a standard press. The ease and quality of the pressed specimens outweighed the expense. My only regret was buying a 5" x 5" press rather than the 9" x 9" model. Follow the instructions that come with the press. ∽

▦ Pressing Vegetables

You can press entire vegetable plants or slices, but you must prepare vegetables so they fit flat into the press.

To press whole plants, choose very young plants or young seedlings. Wash and dry well with paper towels to remove as much moisture as possible. For root vegetables, use a very sharp knife to slice a section from the center of the vegetable, and press with some of the greenery from the top. For beans and mushrooms, take the slices from the center about 1/8" thick. Place the slices into the press between two sheets of thin polyester batting and press. Because of their high moisture content, vegetables take a little longer to dry thoroughly. ∽

FLOWERS & PLANTS SUITABLE FOR PRESSING

Artemisia	Hydrangea (individual blossoms)
Clematis	
Coral bells	Larkspur
Delphiniums	Leaves (all types)
Ferns	Lobelia
Feverfew	Pansies
Forget-me-not	Queen Anne's lace
Freesia	Sweet alyssum
Fuchsia	Violets
Herbs (flowers and leaves)	Wild roses

VEGETABLES SUITABLE FOR PRESSING

Beans	Mushrooms
Beets	Radish
Carrot	

OTHER MATERIALS SUITABLE FOR PRESSING
Grasses
Seaweed and water plants (dry well between paper towels before placing in press)

Using Glycerin

Some leaves and flowers can be preserved with glycerin. The plants soak up the glycerin solution and remain soft and flexible when dried. This is a very useful technique for preserving greenery, as most greenery is very brittle when dried. The disadvantages are that most plants change color (mostly to browns) and they may "sweat" the glycerin solution out after drying. Glycerin also can be expensive; to economize, place the glycerin solution in a small container that can be placed in a larger container to hold the branches upright.

■ How to Preserve with Glycerin

You Will Need:

Greenery	Glycerin (available at drug stores)
Hot water	A sharp knife
A hammer	A container, such as a large vase

Here's How:

1. Harvest plants with a sharp knife and place in a large tub of water while preparing the solution.
2. Mix a solution of 50% hot water and 50% glycerin and place in a large vase. Four cups of prepared solution will treat 10-12 large stems.
3. Remove the bottom leaves from the stems and crush the bottom of the stems with a hammer.
4. Place the stem ends in the solution and leave in a dark, dry location. The stems will soak up the solution and the water will eventually evaporate, leaving the glycerin in the plants. If the plants drink up solution quickly, add more. To lighten the colors, add 1 tablespoon of household bleach to the solution. The plants should be checked after one week, but some plants may take up to three weeks to soak up the solution. When the leaf color has changed, they are ready to hang dry. ∽

PLANTS SUITABLE FOR TREATING WITH GLYCERIN

Baby's breath	Eucalyptus	Maple
Camellia	Holly	Pin Oak
Cedar	Ivy	Salal
Crabapple	Laurel	
Dogwood	Leather fern	

Dehydrating Fruits & Vegetables

Dehydration is the result of drying in a controlled temperature that is high enough to remove moisture from the plant but not so hot as to cook the plant. Good air circulation is important for carrying away the moisture. You can purchase a commercial dehydrator or use your oven.

I prefer to preserve fruits and vegetables by dehydration, but I don't use this method for flowers. Flower petals become brittle when dehydrated—the essential oils and all the moisture are forced out. Citrus peels can be air dried. If you live in an area with very high humidity, you may have no choice but to use a dehydrator for flowers.

■ Using a Commercial Dehydrator

A commercial dehydrator will come with an instruction manual for you to follow. You generally place the thinly sliced fruit or vegetables on the wire mesh trays and place in the dehydrator. The dehydrator is constructed for maximum air circulation with just the right drying temperature. ∽

■ Using Your Oven for Dehydrating

You can successfully dehydrate fruits and vegetables in your home oven.

Here's How::

1. Turn the oven on the lowest possible setting. For better air circulation during drying, take an old tea towel, roll it up, and use it to hold the door open a few inches. The oven temperature is not high, so there is no danger of catching fire. In some ovens, the oven light (or, in a gas stove, the pilot light) produces enough warmth to dry fruit and vegetables.
2. Place clean metal screening on top of the oven racks to lay out the sliced fruit and vegetables. The screens are easily washed after use and can be rolled for storage.
3. Check the drying process every hour and, if needed, turn the slices over so all sides dry evenly. ∽

Fruits Suitable for Dehydrating

Apples, sliced

Citrus fruits (oranges, lemons, limes, grapefruit, kumquat—whole or sliced)

Pears, sliced

Pomegranates, whole or sliced

Star fruit, sliced

Tomatoes, plum variety

Dehydrating Fruits

I usually dry fruits for decoration and crafting purposes. Choose ripe but firm fruits free of blemishes and bruises. Cut fruit into slices 1/4" to 1/8" thick.

Citrus Fruit Slices:

Choose slightly green, thin skinned citrus fruit for drying slices. It cuts more easily and does not contain as much juice.

1. Slice the fruit into slices 1/4" thick and place on three layers of paper towels.
2. Place three more paper towels on top and press the slices to remove as much juice as possible. Repeat this process to remove as much moisture as possible.
3. Place the slices on the dehydrator screen and dry.

Whole Citrus Fruits:

1. Use a carving tool to carve designs into fruit before drying.
2. Push cloves into the fruit in a design for a fragrant pomander. Use an awl to make the holes in the skin before placing the cloves.

In a dehydrator, turn the fruit every hour for the first 5-6 hours to promote even drying and prevent pooling of the juices. The citrus fruits take a very long time to dry. After removing from the dehydrator, place the fruits in a warm, dry area to complete drying.

To air dry: Use a curing mix when air drying whole fruits without the aid of a dehydrator. Mix 2 parts ground cinnamon, 1 part ground cloves, 1/2 part ground allspice, and 1 part powdered orris root. Roll the clove-studded citrus fruit in the mixture for a strong scented fixative.

Citrus Peel:

Citrus peels dry nicely without the use of a dehydrator.
• Cut fruit into quarters and remove the flesh. With a sharp knife, trim away the white membrane. Cut the peel into slices or use a small cookie cutter to cut out shapes. Place on paper towels and dry on top of your refrigerator.
• To make the peel slices dry in a decorative, twisted shape, slightly twist the peel after slicing.
• Use a zester to make long strands of peel. They dry quickly and are decorative in simmers, potpourri, and dried arrangements.

Apples:

• Cut the fruit lengthwise or slice across for a star cut. Cut slices about 1/4" thick. Apple pieces about 1/2" square with the peel on make attractive segments for simmering recipes.
• For fragrant pieces, dredge apple slices or pieces in ground cinnamon or stud with whole cloves before dehydrating. ∽

Dehydrating Vegetables

The vegetables that I dehydrate are those that cost a lot at the store, such as tomatoes and peppers. Choose vegetables that are ripe, firm, and free of blemishes and bruises.

Tomatoes:

• The best tomatoes for drying are the plum type. They are very meaty and firm. I do not peel or de-seed these tomatoes.
• Cut the tomatoes lengthwise into 1/4" slices. Pat the slices gently with a paper towel to dry the excess moisture before placing on the screen.
• Small sweet cherry tomatoes can be dried whole for unique "tomato raisins." ∽

PERSONAL FRAGRANCE CRAFTING

Personal fragrance gifts are immensely popular, thanks to the growing interest in aromatherapy and natural botanical products. A relaxing, scented bath can soothe us and renew our spirits. Many large cosmetic and soap companies spend millions to make their products look homemade.

*It's easy to create natural beauty products from your own garden if you are knowledgeable about the plants' properties and know which botanicals are safe botanicals to use. **Caution: Many herbs can be dangerous to use as bath and beauty products. Pregnant women should avoid using homemade natural products.***

Safe Botanicals & Their Effects

Although no medical claims can be made, essential oils of plants are believed to have pharmacological, physiological, and psychological effects. Here are some of the characteristics attributed to flowers and herbs.

Relaxing: lavender, chamomile, rose, comfrey, lemon verbena, tangerine, sage
Energizing: rosemary, peppermint, bay, jasmine, rose geranium, lemon, lime, lemon balm
Uplifting: orange, jasmine, rosemary
Antiseptic: eucalyptus, peppermint, lavender, tea tree
Soothing for muscle aches: eucalyptus, lavender, rosemary, comfrey, rose, sage
Eases headaches: peppermint, grapefruit, lavender, chamomile
Helps insomnia: chamomile, lavender, mint ∾

Millefiori
Potpourri

Romantic
Bath Herb Blend

Recline and Relax
Bath Herb Blend

Making Facial Scrubs

Facial scrubs made of grated soap and dried botanicals cleanse, stimulate, and soothe the skin. Simple to make and attractive when displayed in a glass jar or in a basket, they're usable potpourri.

▦ Basic Instructions for Facial Scrubs

To make: Gently mix the ingredients in a large bowl. Store in a jar or a basket.
To use: Place 1/4 cup of the blend into a small cotton scrub bag. Tie tightly. Wet the bag well, than rub over your face or body with a gentle circular scrubbing action. Discard contents after use. Rinse the bag with warm water. Lay flat to dry and use again. ৹৹

RECIPES

BEAUTY SCRUB

Oatmeal adds softening effects. Lavender, mint, and sage offer fragrant healing and soothing qualities. This recipe makes 25 applications.

1 cup grated soap (use an unscented beauty bar with added moisturizing cream)
1 cup regular (not instant) oatmeal
1 cup dried lavender buds
1 cup dried mint leaves
1 cup dried sage leaves

PERFUMED SKIN SCRUB

This fragrant mix has a cooling, stimulating effect on your skin. This recipe makes 20 applications.

1 cup grated soap (use a mint scented glycerin soap)
1 cup dried mint leaves
1 cup dried lavender buds
1 cup dried orange peel

Perfumed Skin Scrub

Place 1/4 cup of the blend into the cooton scrub bag. Tie tightly. Wet the bag well, then rub over your face or body with acircular scrubbing action. Rinse Discard the contents after use. Rinse the bag with warm water and lay flat to dry and use again.

Beauty Scrub Facial

Place 1/4 cup of the blend into the cooton scrub bag. Tie tightly. Wet the bag well, then rub over your face or body with acircular scrubbing action. Discard the contents after use. R the bag with warm water and lay dry and use again.

Making Bath Herb Blends

Taking a fragrant herbal bath has become a reliable refuge from the turmoil of everyday life. Be sure to use only plants from the "Safe Botanicals" list in your bath.

▓ Basic Instructions for Bath Herb Blends

To make: Gently mix the ingredients in a large bowl. Store in a jar or a basket. Add 1/4 cup oatmeal (for dry skin) or 1/4 cup cornmeal (for oily skin) to your botanical mixture before simmering for extra scrubbing action.

To use: Place approximately 1/4 cup of the blend in a small cotton bag. Simmer gently in a glass saucepan over medium heat with 1 quart of water for 10 minutes to make a fragrant "tea." Take a quick cleansing shower and draw a tub of water. Pour the "tea" along with its the bag in the bath, hop in, and relax. Use the bag to scrub with. Discard the botanicals when finished. Dry the bag for future use. ∽

RECIPES

RECLINE AND RELAX BATH BLEND

This mix is for when you have nowhere to go and you need a stress-reducing soak in the tub. This recipe makes 16 applications.

1 cup chamomile flowers (relaxing, soothing)
1 cup lavender buds (scent, relaxing, astringent)
1 cup lemon verbena (scent, relaxing)
1 cup strawberry leaves (good for aches and pains)

ROMANTIC BATH BLEND

This is a wonderful calming but energizing blend that leaves your skin scented. This recipe makes 12 applications.

1 cup rose petals (scent, relaxing)
1 cup rose geranium (scent, refines pores, energizing)
1/2 cup lemon balm (scent, stimulating)
1/2 cup chamomile (scent, soothing)

SPARKLING START BATH BLEND

This refreshing and stimulating blend is perfect for the start of your day or to help refresh you after a busy day. This recipe makes 12 applications.

1 cup rosemary (scent and stimulating)
1 cup peppermint leaves (scent, refines pores, astringent, stimulating)
1/2 cup lavender buds (scent, astringent)
1/2 cup sage (eases aching muscles, fresh scent, antiseptic)
1/4 lemon peel (scent, energizing)

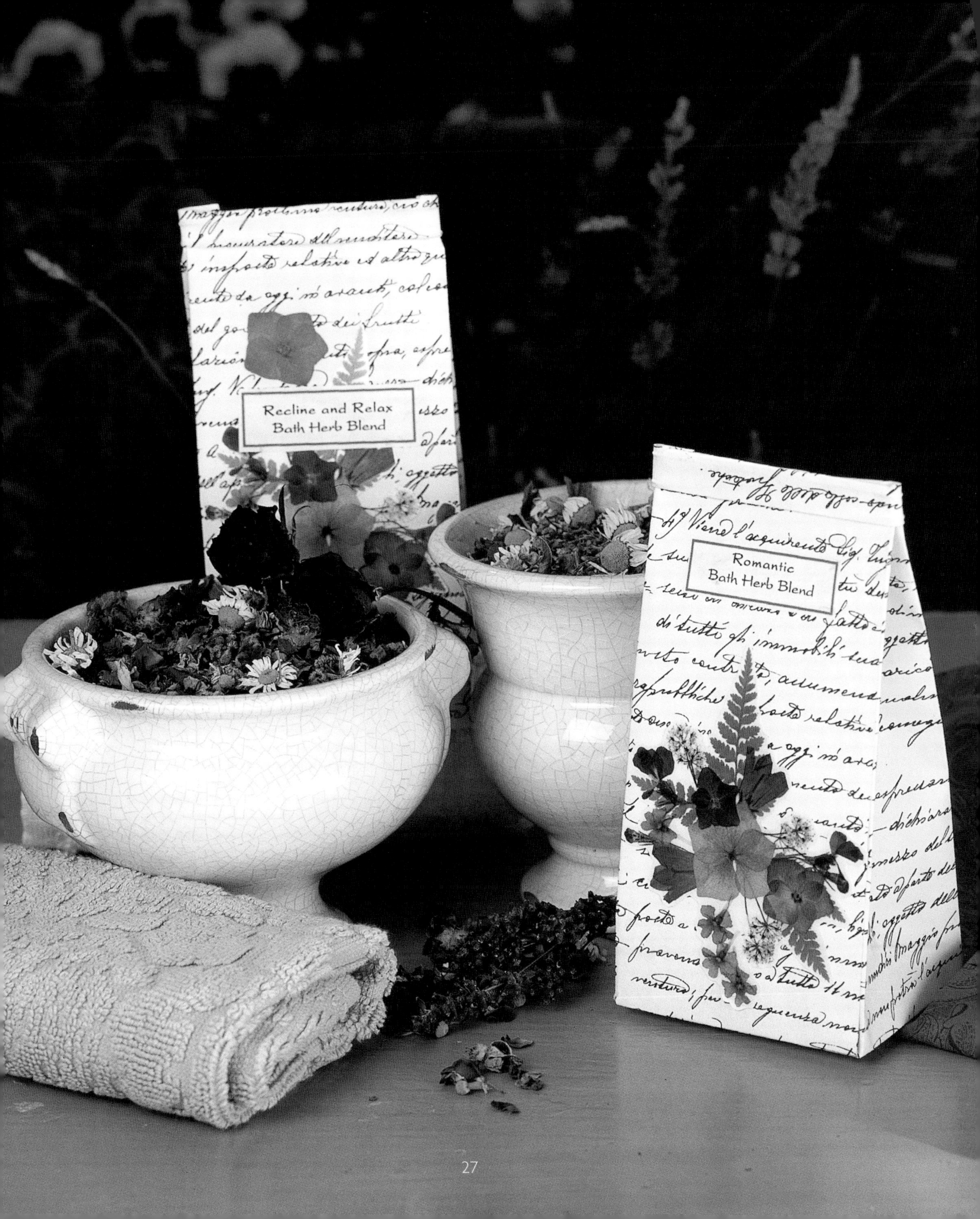
Recline and Relax
Bath Herb Blend
Romantic
Bath Herb Blend

Making Bath Oils

Bath oils soften your skin with a fine film of oil that scents the air as the fragrance is released into the steamy water. They also help soften hard water and look nice when displayed in the bathroom. Botanical bath oils are all the rage in cosmetic departments; here are instructions for creating your own blends for inexpensive, well received gifts.

▒ Basic Bath Oil Blend

You Will Need:
1/2 cup almond oil
1/2 cup castor oil
Oil from 8 vitamin E capsules
1 cup sunflower oil
20 to 30 drops fragrance oil

Here's How:
Mix the oils in a glass jar with a tight-fitting lid. Add the fragrance oils and stir gently to mix. Leave for two weeks, shaking occasionally to allow the scents to mellow. Decant into decorative bottles with dried botanicals. Seal with sealing wax.

- Because homemade bath oils do not contain preservatives, they can become rancid. The addition of vitamin E, an antioxidant, helps the oils last longer, and vitamin E has healing benefits for your skin.
- Botanical bath oils stay sweet for about six months. Always include a "best before" date on your bottle.
- Herbs and flowers can be placed in the bottles before pouring in the oil to add a decorative touch. Use **only fully dried items**; fresh ones will mold and make your oil rancid.

- Use **only** flowers and leaves from the "Safe Botanicals" list in your bath oils. Other safe plant materials, which can be used dried to decorate bath oils, are statice, strawflowers, globe amaranth, pansy, feverfew, and angel wings. **Do not use** commercially dyed flowers in your bath products.
- To color your bath oil, pour 1/8 cup of the base oil in a small glass cup. Shave three to four slivers of solid candle dye into the oil. Microwave on high for 10 seconds. Stir with a wooden stick to blend. Repeat until the dye is melted and evenly distributed. Pour this concentrated mix in with the remaining oils. Let the oils cool before adding fragrance or vitamin E oils.

To Use:
Add 1 tablespoon to your bath water. You also can use this as a massage oil.

Suggested Scented Oil Blends:
Lemon verbena, rose, and orange
Rose, lavender, and lemon
Rosemary, lavender, and peppermint
Lime, lemon, and sandalwood (good blend for men)
Rose, musk, and a tiny bit of cinnamon ∞

MILLEFIORI BATH OIL RECIPE

To the Basic Bath Oil Blend, add these floral fragrance oils:

10 drops rose
5 drops violet
5 drops honeysuckle

Add these dried flowers to the bottles before adding oils:
Small pink rose buds
Peach, blue, and yellow statice blossoms
Small white strawflowers

STIMULATING BATH OIL RECIPE

To the Basic Bath Oil Blend, add these fragrance oils:

10 drops peppermint
10 drops orange

Add these dried materials to the bottles before adding the oils:
Mint leaves
Small white strawflowers
Yellow rose petals
Dried orange peel

Making Floral Waters

Soothing, fragrant, decorative floral waters are both convenient and inexpensive to make. Use as a refreshing after bath splash or a mild astringent, spritz for an air freshener, or uncover and let the fragrance refresh a room.

▒ Types of Floral Waters

Alcohol-based floral waters: Alcohol-based floral waters are made by combining fresh botanicals with a grain alcohol (vodka) and letting them sit for a few weeks to scent and color the liquid. Use only glass jars with non-metallic lids. The solution is then strained and fragrance oils are dissolved in the scented alcohol. This fragrant mix is added to distilled water to dilute the finished product. Dried botanicals can be added to the bottles for decoration, if you wish.

Vinegar-based floral waters: Another type of floral water is made from fresh botanicals and vinegar. Vinegar-based floral waters make fine astringents for your face and also may be added to bath water. Fresh botanicals are soaked in vinegar for three weeks (or until all the color and fragrance has been leached out). Use only glass jars with non-metallic lids. I sometimes strain the mixture, add additional fresh botanicals, and soak an additional three weeks to make an extra-fragrant blend. The mixture is then diluted with distilled water or rose water. No additional fragrance oils are added. ∾

RECIPES

LAVENDER & ROSE FLORAL WATER

Mix 1/4 cup fresh lavender buds and 1/4 cup red rose petals with 1/2 cup vodka (or enough to cover) in a jar. Let stand covered in a cool, dark place for two weeks. Decant and strain the mixture. Add 10 drops rose oil and 5 drops lavender oil, stirring gently to dissolve the oils. Add 3 cups distilled water. Let stand an additional week for the scents to mellow. Pour into a decorative bottle with sprigs of dried lavender and dried rose petals for decoration.

ORANGE SPICE WATER

Mix the rind of one orange and 10 whole allspice berries with 1/4 cup vodka in a jar. Let stand, covered, for two to three weeks in a dark, cool place. Decant and strain the mixture. Add 15 drops sweet orange oil and stir to dissolve. Add 3 cups distilled water. Let the scents mellow for another week. Pour into decorative bottles with a few allspice berries and a long strip of dried orange zest for decoration.

FAIRY WATER

Gently heat 1 cup apple cider vinegar. Pour over 1/4 cup fresh red rose petals, 1/4 cup mint leaves, and 1/8 cup sage leaves. Place in a covered jar and let stand, shaking daily, for two weeks. Decant and strain the mixture. Add 1/2 cup rose water to the vinegar. Decant into decorative bottles.

HOME FRAGRANCE CRAFTING

Home fragrance products help to dispel musty odors in dresser drawers, closed luggage, and closed up homes during the cold winter months. Using natural products to clean and scent your home makes housework a little more pleasant.
In this section are recipes for creating potpourri, simmering potpourri, sachets, air fresheners, and scented cleaners and ideas for fragrant fires. Imagine yourself in a 17th century "still room," where the lady of the manor dried and pre-pared botanicals for her household.

Making Potpourri

Potpourri is a scented blend of dried petals and spices with aromatic oils stabilized by fixatives. Making potpourri is a creative, fun, and simple way to capture the beauty and fragrances of your summer garden for display the whole year round.

The word potpourri comes from the French word *pourrie*, which means "to rot." Originally, potpourri was made by the moist method—partially dried plant material was layered with salt and spices to preserve the fragrances. This pickled floral mixture would be cured throughout the summer as new fragrant flowers came into season. Spices, fixatives, and ingredients such as brown sugar and brandy would be mixed in to create highly fragrant mixtures that

lasted up to 50 years! The moist potpourri created was an unsightly mixture of limp brown petals that was kept in a opaque jar. The jar's lid was removed whenever the room needed to be refreshed.

Today, the dry method is more popular, as it is quicker and easier to make. Dry potpourris are beautiful to display, and the recipes in this book are made by the dry method. Ingredients for dry potpourri include dry plant materials, fixatives, and fragrant oils. You can easily create buckets of your own blends for gift giving using these recipes. A properly blended dry potpourri with fixatives can last up to two years—even longer if refreshed.

This photo shows a variety of potpourri you can make and package for special gifts. See the following pages for a look at how each blend is made.

▨ Botanicals

Many botanicals can be used in creating potpourri. Plant materials can be divided into three groups: main scent, blenders, and bulk. All plant materials need to be fully dried before blending.

The **main scent** is the key scent. Because very few plant materials, with the exception of some roses, lavender, and herbs, keep their scents after they are dried, the actual scent usually is supplied by the addition of fragrant oils. However, when you create a potpourri blend made up mostly of rose petals, the botanical used determines what fragrant oils will be used. Other scents are added to modify and enhance the main scent.

The **blenders** are plant materials that add a scent, but not as strong as the main scent. Blenders give harmony and maintain the balance of the blend, as a single scent is not as lasting or as endearing as a blended scent. Even a rose blend benefits from blenders such as spices, to give a pleasant, lasting note. The aromatic fixatives can also add the blender scents to a mix.

Botanicals (cont.)

Bulk is any plant material that adds color, texture, interest, or extra bulk to the potpourri blend. Some bulk is not even botanical, such as the gold leaf in the Gift of Kings Potpourri or the gingerbread stars in the Yuletide Star Potpourri.

Fragrant Oils

Fragrant oils are a significant part of creating potpourri blends, and many different fragrant oils are available. There are two basic types: essential oils and fragrance oils.

Essential oils are the natural extracts of botanicals. Essential oils are very popular today, thanks in part to the growing interest in aromatherapy. Many fruits, spices, and plants such as eucalyptus and lavender yield pure essential oils at a reasonable cost.

Fragrance oils are synthetic products that were developed in the 1950s to replace natural essential oils. It is not now possible to extract the essence from many botanicals because of the cost and shrinking availability. Unless you are paying over $50 an ounce, your rose or jasmine oil will be a fragrance oil or a blended oil (a blend of essential and fragrance oils).

Both fragrance oils and essential oils are used in potpourri. When you purchase fragrance oils, scents closest to nature are the best. Let your nose decide. Do not buy cheap oils or extracts; you will be disappointed. Carry a bag of freshly ground coffee with you when sniffing oils to help clear your nose.

Fixatives

It is the nature of fragrance and essential oils to evaporate. Without the surrounding cell structure of the plant to contain it, scent quickly dissipates into the air. Materials that take the place of the plant's cell structure, therefore slowing the evaporating process, are known as fixatives. Fixatives contribute their own scents and help blend, clarify, and enhance the other fragrant elements of potpourri.

Animal fixatives that were popular in the past are no longer used in the interest of ecology. (Ambergris from the sperm whale nearly made the species extinct.) Now only vegetable fixatives are used.

Effective Plant-derived Fixatives:
Orris root (available in powdered or chip forms)
Sandalwood   Oak Moss
Calamus root   Frankincense and myrrh

Less Effective Plant-derived Fixatives:

Tonka beans	Allspice	Nutmeg
Coriander seeds	Cinnamon	Citrus peel
Dill	Cloves	

Fibre-fix:
About ten years ago, ground corncobs appeared on the market as fixatives called "fibre-fix" or "cellulose fibre." They were cheaper and said to be free of substances that can cause allergic reactions. However, when a ground corn product is used as a potpourri fixative, two or three times the amount of fragrant oils is required. Since oils are the most costly ingredient in potpourri, I don't use these fixatives.

Basic Fragrant Fixative Blend:
This blend is an effective and fragrant fixative. Blend all the ingredients and use in place of any fixative in potpourri recipes.

1 cup orris root	1/2 cup allspice
1 cup cinnamon chips	1/4 cup frankincense
1/2 cup whole cloves	1/4 cup myrrh
1/2 cup sandalwood	

How To Make Dry Potpourri

You Will Need:
6 cups dried plant material (1 cup main scent, 2 cups blenders, 3 cups bulk)
2 heaping tablespoons fixative
10 to 20 drops fragrant oil

continued on next page

Making Potpourri

continued from page 33

Here's How:

1. Gently mix all botanicals in a large glass bowl until the appearance pleases you. Add bits of bulk to brighten and add color.
2. Let the botanical mixture mellow for a few days in a closed container. Adjust ingredients if needed.
3. Mix the fragrant oils with the fixatives in a glass jar. Let the scents mellow and blend overnight. This makes sure all the oils have been soaked up by the fixatives.
4. Mix the botanicals with the blended fixatives and oils. Let the mixture cure for two to three weeks in a sealed container. Stir occasionally to blend.
5. Add ingredients to change or improve the scent, if desired. Keep a record as you work. If you create a successful blend, you will want to reproduce it.

To use: Never display potpourri in the direct sunlight, which fades the colors and evaporates the fragrance oils. Display in simple bowls or containers to show off the colors and textures.

How to Refresh Old Potpourri:

- Refresh old potpourri by adding more fragrant oils. Shake the fixatives to the bottom of the bowl. Remove the fixatives and add the oils directly to them. Let mellow overnight before adding back to the blend.

- Simply crushing or mixing the blend releases the fragrance. You also can sprinkle a little brandy on potpourri to refresh it.
- Never add fresh or partially dried plant materials to finished potpourri. Add only fully dried botanicals to refresh the color and scent. ∾

Making Cinnamon Ginger Stars

These fragrant stars are a great addition to potpourri. They also can be used as ornaments or glued to craft projects.

Mix together in a plastic bag:

1/2 cup powdered cinnamon	1 teaspoon ground cloves
1 tablespoon powdered ginger	1 teaspoon ground nutmeg

In a small bowl, mix together:

3/8 cup smooth applesauce	1 tablespoon white craft glue

Add the applesauce mixture to the bag. Close the bag and squeeze to mix until the mixture forms a ball. Take out and knead on a cinnamon-sprinkled surface. Roll out the dough to a 1/4" thickness and cut into shapes with small cookie cutters. For ornaments, use a straw to make a hole before drying. Let the stars dry slowly, turning them frequently. ∾

YULETIDE STAR POTPOURRI RECIPE

This is a fun Christmas blend with many surprises! Use dried cranberries in place of the rose hips for a brighter red.

Ingredients:

Botanicals:
1/2 cup rose hips
1/2 cup broken cinnamon sticks
1/2 cup small pine cones
1/4 cup dried orange stars
1/4 cup whole star anise
1 tablespoon each: whole cloves and
   whole allspice

Accents:
12 miniature cinnamon ginger stars
   (recipe follows)

Fixative: 1 tablespoon Sandalwood
Fragrant Oils: 10 drops cinnamon oil

Here's How: Mix according to instructions for Basic Potpourri. Let cure two weeks. Makes approximately 5 cups.

GIFT OF KINGS POTPOURRI RECIPE

This is another Christmas blend that includes the ingredients presented by the three wise men. You also can make a simple but elegant blend of frankincense, myrrh, gold leaf, and a few drops of Christmas oil.

Ingredients:
Botanicals:
2 cups dried red rose petals
1 cup rose hips, 1 cup mini pine cones
1 cup oak moss
2 cups balsam pine needles or cedar tips
1/4 cup allspice
Accents: 1 crumpled sheet gold leaf
Fixatives:
1 tablespoon frankincense
1 tablespoon myrrh
Fragrant Oils:
15 drops tea rose oil
5 drops cinnamon oil

Here's How: Mix according to instructions for Basic Potpourri. Let cure four weeks. Makes approximately 7 cups.

LEMON LACE POTPOURRI RECIPE

Ingredients:
Botanicals:
1/2 cup lemon slices
1 cup whole yellow or white roses
1 cup sunflower petals
1 cup yellow rose petals
1 cup lemon verbena
1/2 cup white angel wings
Accent:
Dried lemon slices tied into bundles
    with natural raffia
Fixative:
1 heaping tablespoon orris root
Fragrant Oils:
10 drops rose oil
10 drops lemon oil

Here's How: Mix according to instructions for Basic Potpourri. Let cure four weeks. Makes approximately 5 cups.

ROSE BOWL
POTPOURRI RECIPE

This is an old fashioned looking rose potpourri.

Ingredients:

Botanicals:
2 cups pink rose petals and buds
1 cup red rose petals
1 cup pink flower petals (larkspur, peony, or bougainvillea)
1/2 cup oak moss
2 tablespoons whole cloves
Accent:
Dried whole roses
Fixative:
2 heaping tablespoons orris root
Fragrant Oils:
10 drops rose oil
8 drops lavender oil

Here's How: Mix according to instructions for Basic Potpourri. Let cure four weeks. Makes approximately 5 cups.

WOODLAND WALK
POTPOURRI RECIPE

Ingredients:

Botanicals:
1 cup balsam pine needles
1/2 cup broken cinnamon sticks
1/4 cup small pine cones
1/2 cup curly pods
1/2 cup baby wood roses
1/2 cup hibiscus flowers
1 tablespoon juniper berries
1 tablespoon rosemary sprigs
1 tablespoon rose hips
1 tablespoon oak moss
1 tablespoon star anise
Accent: Pine cones and seed pods
Fixative:
1 heaping tablespoon Fragrant Fixative Blend
Fragrant Oil:
20 drops rainforest oil

Here's How: Mix according to instructions for Basic Potpourri. Let cure four weeks. Makes approximately 5 cups.

TAPESTRY POTPOURRI RECIPE

Ingredients:
Botanicals:
1 cup hibiscus flowers
1 cup red rose petals
1 cup dark blue delphinium petals
1/2 cup lemon verbena
1/2 cup cranberry colored Milo berries
1 tablespoon star anise
Accent:
Gilded bay leaves
Fixative:
1-1/2 heaping tablespoons Fragrant
    Fixative Blend
Fragrant Oils:
10 drops jasmine
10 drops vanilla

Here's How: Mix according to instructions for Basic Potpourri. Let cure three weeks. Makes approximately 4 cups.

MILLEFIORI POTPOURRI RECIPE

This potpourri blend is much like a clean-out-the-refrigerator stew. At the end of the summer, you may have a lot of flowers left over from fragrance crafting that can be blended in this mix. Remember, nothing in nature clashes, so anything goes! Millefiori means a "thousand flowers." Make a lot!

Ingredients:
Botanicals:
Dried petals and blossoms to make 6 cups
1 cup lemon verbena leaves (The
    green helps show off the many colors in this blend.)
Fixative:
2 heaping tablespoons Fragrant
    Fixative Blend
Fragrant Oils:
10 drops rose oil, 5 drops honeysuckle oil
5 drops sweet violet oil

Here's How: Mix according to instructions for Basic Potpourri. Let cure two weeks. Makes approximately 7 cups.

BLUE BOWL POTPOURRI RECIPE

This is a single color blend with a refreshing scent.

Ingredients:
Botanicals:
1 cup light blue delphinium petals
1 cup dark blue delphinium petals
1 cup lavender
1/2 cup blue larkspur
1/2 cup hydrangea petals
1/2 cup white angel wings
1/2 cup juniper berries
Fixative:
1 tablespoon orris root
Fragrant Oils:
10 drops peppermint oil
10 drops lavender oil

Here's How: Mix according to instructions for Basic Potpourri. Let cure three weeks. Makes approximately 5 cups.

SEA MIST POTPOURRI RECIPE

This recipe is my favorite. It looks beautiful displayed in the bathroom in a large sea shell.

Ingredients:
Botanicals:
1 cup blue flower petals (delphinium, cornflower, larkspur)
2 cups nigella pods
1/2 cup lavender buds and leaves
1/4 cup rosemary
1/4 cup willow eucalyptus leaves
1/4 cup oak moss
Accent:
Lavender bundles tied with raffia and sea shells
Fixative: 1 tablespoon orris root
Fragrant oils:
10 drops peppermint oil
5 drops lavender oil
2 drops eucalyptus oil

Here's How: Mix according to instructions for Basic Potpourri. Let cure three weeks, Makes approximately 5 cups.

Making Simmering Potpourri

Simmering potpourris or simmers are popular because they quickly fill the house with fragrance. They are specially formulated to be visually appealing and aromatic.

Simmers also can kill germs associated with a cold or flu. Effective air cleansing botanicals include clove, cinnamon, sage, eucalyptus, lemon, peppermint, rosemary, lavender, and thyme.

I use only sandalwood as the fixative, as many people are sensitive to orris root.

To make: Simmering potpourris are blended in the same way as dry potpourris, but the bulk material is omitted and only fragrant botanicals are used.

To use: Add approximately 3 tablespoons of the blend to 1 quart of simmering water in a glass saucepan. Reduce heat to a gentle simmer, adding hot water as needed. Do not let the mixture come to a full boil. Discard the simmered mixture after use. ∞

APPLE SPICE SIMMERING POTPOURRI

Ingredients:
Botanicals:
2 cups apple slices
1 cup cinnamon pieces
1/2 cup chamomile
1/2 cup orange peel
1/4 cup allspice
1/4 cup star anise
1/4 cup bay leaves
1 vanilla bean, chopped
1/4 cup sage leaves
1 tablespoon whole cloves
1 tablespoon whole cardamom
Fixative:
1/2 cup sandalwood
Fragrant Oils:
10 drops green apple oil
8 drops cinnamon oil

Here's How: Mix according to instructions for Basic Potpourri. Let cure two weeks. Makes approximately 5 cups.

CITRUS SPICE SIMMERING POTPOURRI

Ingredients:
Botanicals:
2 cups orange peel
1 cup citrus slices
1/2 cup bay leaf
1/2 cup tilia flowers
1/2 cup sunflower petals
1/4 cup allspice
1/4 cup star anise
1/4 cup cinnamon pieces
1 tablespoon whole cloves
Accent:
Bundles of orange slices tied with raffia
Fixative:
1 heaping tablespoon sandalwood
Fragrant Oils:
10 drops sweet orange oil
5 drops lemon oil
5 drops cinnamon oil

Here's How: Mix according to instructions for Basic Potpourri. Let cure two weeks. Makes approximately 5 cups.

CHRISTMAS TREE SIMMERING POTPOURRI RECIPE

I use the dried needles from our balsam fir Christmas tree to make this blend. To identify a balsam fir, feel the needles; they will be soft, not sharp. The needles are flat and, when fresh, smell like strong tangerines.

Ingredients:
Botanicals:
1 cup mini pine cones, 1 cup rose hips
3/4 cup balsam fir needles
1/4 cup rosemary, 1/4 cup bay leaves
1/2 cup sage, 1/4 cup whole cloves
1/4 cup broken cinnamon sticks
1/4 cup hibiscus, 1/4 cup orange peel
Fixative: 3 tablespoons sandalwood
Fragrant Oils:
10 drops cinnamon oil
5 drops orange oil

Here's How: Mix according to instructions for Basic Potpourri. Let cure three weeks. Makes approximately 4 cups.

INVIGORATING & FRESH SIMMERING POTPOURRI RECIPE

This air freshening simmer does not use any added oils, so it's very economical to make.

Ingredients:
Botanicals:
1 cup peppermint leaves
1/2 cup rosemary
1/4 cup cloves
1/4 cup lemon peel
Fixative:
1 tablespoon sandalwood

Here's How: Mix according to instructions for Basic Potpourri. Let cure two weeks. Makes approximately 5 cups.

MINTY CITRUS SIMMERING POTPOURRI RECIPE

Ingredients:
Botanicals:
2 cups mint leaves
1 cup orange, lemon and lime peel
1 cup lemon verbena
1 tablespoon juniper berries
1 tablespoon allspice
Fixative:
1 tablespoon sandalwood
Fragrant Oils:
10 drops peppermint
5 drops each of sweet orange and lemon

Here's How: Mix according to instructions for Basic Potpourri. Let cure two weeks. Makes approximately 4 cups.

Making Sachets

Sachets are dry potpourri blends that have been finely chopped and mixed with a filler to go into bags and pillows. The color of a sachet is not as important (unless you are using a sheer fabric) as the fragrance and the properties of the botanicals. The recipes in this section include blends to help you sleep, discourage bugs, freshen linens, and keep you alert at the computer.

Sachet fillers can be any unscented material that helps to fill out the sachet. I prefer buckwheat hulls, but cornstarch also works well. All the botanicals are coarsely crushed or processed in a blender until finely chopped. Use a mortar and pestle or spice grinder for the hard spices and a old blender for the leaves and petals.

To make paper sachets, simply decorate an envelope with rubber stamps or stencils, fill with your sachet blend, and seal. You can also create beautiful envelope sachets from decorative papers by taking an envelope apart carefully and using it as a template. ∞

SHUT-EYE SACHET RECIPE

Blend:
1 cup chamomile
1 cup mint
1 cup sweet woodruff
1 cup rose geranium
Add:
1 cup buckwheat hulls
Optional: 1 cup dried hops
Use: Let mellow in a closed container for one week. Replace after six months of use.

LINEN SACHET RECIPE

Fill sachets with this blend and tuck into your closet to keep your linens smelling fresh. Or place this mix into pretty paper envelopes, sealed tight, for a lovely gift to tuck inside a suitcase.

Blend:
1/2 cup finely ground lemon peel
1 tablespoon crushed coriander
1 tablespoon grated nutmeg
1 tablespoon crushed whole cloves
1/4 cup lavender buds
Mix & Add:
1 teaspoon powdered orris root
1/2 cup cornstarch

CRITTER GONE SACHET RECIPE

Keeps bugs away.
Blend:
1 cup cedar chips
1 cup lavender
Add:
1 tablespoon coarsely ground black pepper
1/4 cup coarsely chopped cinnamon sticks
1/4 cup ground cloves
Add:
1/2 cup vermiculite (found in garden centers)
10 drops lavender oil
Use: Let mellow for 1 week. This blend can be scattered on a rug, left for a day, and then vacuumed up. Leave the blend in your vacuum bag, and you will get a shot of fragrance every time you vacuum that is pleasant to us but not pleasant to bugs.

COMPUTER COMPANION SACHET RECIPE

This energizing blend clears head, eases eye strain, and keeps you alert at your computer.

Blend:
1 cup lavender buds
1 cup peppermint leaves
1 cup lemon verbena
1/2 cup sage leaves
Mix & Blend:
10 drops peppermint oil
5 drops lavender oil
1 teaspoon of powdered orris root
Add:
1/2 cup buckwheat hulls
Use: Let mellow for one week before filling your sachets.

SAVON ESS·VIOLETTE
de L.T. PIVER
10 BOULEVARD DE STRASBOURG
PARIS

Linen
Sachet

SAVON AU P

Making Pomanders

Pomanders are clove-studded fruits that were dried, cured, and carried about during the Middle Ages when general sanitation was not what it is today. Pomanders could be quite elaborate, depending on one's position in society.

◼ How to Make Wax Pomanders

Another type of pomander is a wax sachet blend that is covered with dried rose buds, lavender buds, or chopped flower petals.

You Will Need:
1 ounce beeswax
1/2 cup smooth applesauce
1 cup ground cinnamon
1 tablespoon ground ginger
1 tablespoon ground nutmeg
1 tablespoon ground allspice
10 drops of fragrant oil (use rose oil if covering with rose-buds, lavender oil if rolling in lavender buds, etc.)
Dried rosebuds OR dried lavender buds OR whole cloves

Here's How:
1. Heat the wax and applesauce in a container over a hot water bath until the wax is melted.

2. Stir in the ground spices. Let the mixture cool.
3. Pour out the mixture on a piece of wax paper, a piece of aluminum foil, or a marble surface. Knead until well mixed and smooth.
4. Roll small balls in your palm about 2" in diameter. Set aside.
5. While the mixture is still soft, push in whole cloves or rosebuds to decorate or roll sachet in lavender buds.
6. Let air dry until hard, 3 to 4 days. The fragrance will last for years. ◡

◼ How To Make Citrus Pomanders

I love citrus fruits, carved with designs and studded decoratively with whole cloves, for making pomanders. To make them, follow the instructions in the section on dehydrating whole citrus fruits. ◡

Knead wax mixture until smooth.

Roll sachet balls in lavender buds.

Making Scented Cleaners

Give your home a fragrant lift with natural cleaning products. They are safer to use than harsh commercial products and a lot easier on the pocketbook!

SCENTED CLEANING POWDER RECIPE

This non-scratching powder is suitable for cleaning tubs, sinks, and counter tops.

Grind together in a spice grinder or with a mortar and pestle:

1 tablespoon dried orange peel
1 tablespoon dried lavender
1 tablespoon balsam fir needles.

Add:

1/2 cup baking soda
1/2 cup borax

Mix in:

10 drops lemon fragrance oil

Use: Let mellow a few days before using.

CARPET FRESHENER RECIPE

When the carpet smells musty, sprinkle it with this blend. Leave for a few hours, then vacuum up. The herbs add fragrance and deodorize the carpet, deterring moths, fleas, and pet smells.

Mix:

3 cups lavender buds
2 cups rosemary leaves
2 cups baking soda

AIR FRESHENER SPRAY RECIPE

This blend freshens and disinfects the air to inhibit the growth of micro-organisms.

Mix:

1/2 cup fresh lavender buds
1/2 cup fresh mint leaves
1 tablespoon whole cloves

Steep:

Steep in 1/2 cup vodka (or enough to cover). Let stand for two weeks, shaking daily. Decant and strain.

Add:

5 drops lavender oil   5 drops peppermint oil
8 drops tea tree oil

Stir until the oils have dissolved. Mix with 1 cup distilled water.

Use: Place mixture in a spray bottle. Avoid spraying around people's faces or on fine furniture. *See section on Floral Waters for additional fragrant spray recipes.*

CITRUS MINT WINDOW SPRAY RECIPE

Mix:

1/2 cup fresh lemon peel
1/2 cup fresh orange peel
1 cup fresh mint leaves

Steep:

Steep in 1 cup white vinegar. Let stand for two weeks or until vinegar has leached out the color and fragrance of the botanicals.

Use: Decant and strain. Place in a spray bottle. Use to clean your windows to a sparking shine.

Critter Gone Sachet

...net on your ...and leave overnight ...
...we the ...h your vacuum and ...

Citrus Mint Window Spray

Scented Cleaning Powder

Making Fire Starters

There is nothing quite as nice cuddling up around a fireplace for a relaxing evening. These blends are ideas for making fragrant and beautiful fires.

CAUTION: Please use caution whenever you have a fire. **Never** leave a fire unattended. **Never** place combustibles near a fireplace. **Do not use these products in a closed stove or fireplace.**

▨ Fragrant Fire Bundles

After harvesting fragrant herbs and flowers, you are left with a pile of stripped stems. Gather stems from sage, lavender, rosemary, mint, eucalyptus, and scented geraniums. Bundle and tie together with natural raffia. Toss on your fire to add a pleasant, natural scent. ∽

▨ Pine Cone Fire Starters

Use these fragrant waxed cones for decoration and to quickly start a blaze in the fireplace.

You Will Need:

Pine cones   Candle dye OR old crayons
Paraffin   Candle fragrance
Candle wicking

Here's How:

1. Melt the paraffin wax in a double boiler.
2. Add candle dye (old crayons can be used) and candle fragrance to the melted wax.
3. Cut a piece of candle wicking 12" long. Tie one end around the base of the cone and the other end to another cone. (You will now have two cones connected with a piece of wick.) Dip the cones one by one in the melted wax until you are happy with the coverage.
4. Prop a yardstick or broom handle between two chairs. Cover the floor underneath with newspaper to catch drips. Hang the cones over the yardstick or broom handle. Let dry.
5. Trim the wicking so there is a 2" fuse on each cone.

Use:

Display your fragrant cones in a basket near the fireplace (not so close that sparks could ignite them). **To use:** Place one cone in the fireplace and light the wick to quickly start your fire. ∽

▨ Yule Log

A dried flower yule log makes a welcome gift. This project can be done outside using fresh cedar boughs and pine cones pushed into the wax. If you wish to add a bow, use inexpensive paper ribbon.

CAUTION! This arrangement is **for fireplace use only**. Never, ever light the candle without first placing the log safely inside the fireplace. The candle will burn, the dried plants will catch fire, and soon you'll have a roaring blaze.

You Will Need:

A log   Pillar candle
Paraffin wax   Dried plant material
Optional: Thick craft glue, paper ribbon

Here's How:

1. Place some wax on the stove in the top of a double boiler.
2. When the wax is melted, remove from the stove and gently mix until lumpy.
3. Place the warm wax on the top of the log. Place a pillar candle in the middle of the log. (The wax will hold the candle in place.)
4. Push dried plant material into the wax to create an arrangement. If the wax hardens before you are finished, glue the material in place with thick craft glue. ∽

▨ Rainbow Fire Cones

My father made these cones when I was a child, and I remember staring into the ever changing colors of the fire—truly a gift of a wonderful memory.

You Will Need:

A large plastic pail   Water   A wooden stick
Pine cones   Chemicals (see below)

Here's How:

1. Put 1 gallon warm water in a large plastic pail.
2. Dissolve the chemical in the water, stirring with wooden stick.
For yellow-green flames: One pound copper sulfate (from garden supply centers or hardware stores) will treat 30 medium-size cones.
For blue-green flames: 1/2 pound boric acid (from drugstores) will treat 16 large cones.
For orange-yellow flames: 1-1/2 pounds rock salt (from the grocery store) will treat 24 small cones.
3. Submerge the pine cones. (You may need to use a plate with a rock on top to keep them under the water.) Allow the cones to soak for 6-7 days, stirring the mixture every day.
4. Remove the cones. Spread on newspaper to dry. They will open as they dry. They may take several weeks to dry completely.
5. Package cones in burlap bags or wooden crates.

Use: Toss a cone into the fire for a dancing dazzle of fiery color. ∽

FIRE
STARTERS

PLACE A PINE CONE IN THE
FIREPLACE AND LIGHT THE
WICK TO QUICKLY START A
COZY FIRE.

CULINARY CRAFTING

Crafting delicious meals from the garden is a pleasure, and presenting favorite recipes as gifts is a wonderful way to share the bounty of your garden. Packaging and presentation play a large part in your gift's appeal, and good recipes and sound preserving techniques will give the recipients chef quality, professional results.

Included in the pages that follow are recipes for making and using herb blends, fruit and herb butters, herbal and fruit vinegars, herbal oils, flavored sugars, honey, and syrups, teas, spirited fruits and liquors, and biscuit and muffin mixes. They are simple to create and package, delicious and easy for the recipients to prepare.

Pictured at right: *Edible flowers are used in salads and to decorate cheeses. See page 52 for a listing of edible flowers.*

Edible Flowers

Most of the herbs in our garden have flowers that are edible, as do some pretty border plants. Not only are the flowers beautiful, they also are flavorful, with a mild, but similar taste to that of their leaves. Fancy restaurants use colorful blossoms as garnishes and as the main flavoring ingredient in many dishes. You can too! As you become familiar to flavoring with flowers, try adding them to your favorite recipes to enhance and give them extraordinary new flavor.

When using flowers in culinary crafting, always follow these rules:

- Eat **only** flowers you know to be safe.
- Eat **only** flowers you know are free of herbicides and pesticides.
- **Do not eat** flowers from plants that grow along the roadside.
- Remove the hard pistils and stamens—eat **only the petals**.
- Rinse blossoms under water and dry them before using in your recipes.

How to Make Sugared Flowers

Tiny candied flowers are a beautiful garnish for simple cakes and desserts. Making sugared flowers is easy, and they will last five to six months.

Choose fresh, perfect blossoms that are clean and dry, such as miniature roses, violets, pansies, borage, scented geranium leaves, mint leaves, and lemon balm leaves. Use only powdered egg white, so there is no danger of salmonella poisoning from uncooked eggs.

You Will Need:

Powdered egg white
Superfine granulated sugar, sometimes called "berry sugar" (or use a scented or flavored sugar)
Small, clean paint brush (Use for this purpose only.)
A shaker   Wax paper   Edible flowers with a short stem
Drying screen (I use an embroidery hoop with a piece of window screening)

Here's How:

1. In a small bowl, place 1 teaspoon powdered egg white and 1 tablespoon water. Mix well with a fork. Skim off any foam or undissolved powder. Fill a clean shaker with sugar.
2. With a paint brush, cover both sides of the blossom with the egg white mixture **(photo 1)**. Holding the flower by its stem over wax paper, immediately sprinkle the flower with sugar, making sure sugar gets in between all the petals **(photo 2)**.
3. Place the sugared blossom on the drying screen and let dry, turning every few hours for even drying. Let blossoms air dry in a dark, dry, well-ventilated area for a few weeks until completely dry. Store in airtight jars in a dark, dry area. ∽

EDIBLE FLOWERS FROM THE HERB GARDEN

These flowers are safe for use in recipes for scented sugars and butters and flavored vinegars, syrups, and honey.

Anise Hyssop (*Agastache foeniculum*)
Basil (*Ocimum basilicum*)
Bee balm (*Monarda didyma*)
Borage (*Borago officinalis*)
Chamomile (*Chamaemelum nobile*)
Chives (*Allium schoenoprasum*)
Cilantro (*Coriandrum sativum*)
Dill (*Anethum graveolens*)
Fennel (*Foeniculum vulgare*)
Garlic chives (*Allium tuberosum*)
Lemon verbena (*Aloysia triphylla*)
Marjoram (*Origanum majorana*)
Mint (*Mentha spp.*)
Oregano (*Origanum spp.*)
Rosemary (*Rosmarinus officinalis*)
Sage (*Salvia officinalis*)
Scented geranium (*Pelargonium spp.*)
Thyme (*Thymus spp.*)

EDIBLE BLOSSOMS FROM THE FLOWER GARDEN

Calendula (*Calendula officinalis*)
Honeysuckle (*Lonicera japonica*)
Jasmine (*Jasminum sambac*)
Johnny jump-up (*Viola tricolor*)
Lavender (*Lavandula spp.*)
Nasturtium (*Tropaeolum majus*)
Pansy (*Viola Xwittrockiana*)
Rose (*Rosa spp.*)
Sweet violet (*Viola odorata*)

Making Herb Blends

Herb blends are the most versatile and varied products you can create from your garden. The process is simple, and the results are delicious. Herb blends are easy to package creatively and offer endless possibilities to even novice cooks.

To prepare dried herb blends, first follow the instructions for hang drying and screen drying your harvest. Remember that herbs have the strongest flavors if harvested right before they flower. After the herbs have dried completely, remove the leaves from the stems. If you were to individually strip the leaves from each stem, it would be a laborious task—it's much easier to simply place the whole dried bundle between your palms and rub your hands together over a large bowl. The dried leaves (and some stem pieces) will fall into the bowl. Pick out any large stems, and carefully sift the herbs through a large sieve to remove smaller stems. (I also use flat, tightly woven trays to shake the herbs in to remove any small particles.)

When the herbs are rubbed and sifted, you're ready to create your blends. Use a spice mill or a mortar and pestle to coarsely grind hard spices and peels. I have also used many products from the market including spices, onion and garlic granules, sugars and cheese powders. The recipes have been presented with measurements listed in parts, so you will be able to mix up any quantity you wish. Blend the herbs in a large glass bowl. Package your blends in airtight cellophane bags or glass bottles or jars and store in a dark, cool area. Herb blends last about a year before the flavors and colors fade. ∞

R E C I P E S

LEMON CLOVE HERB BLEND

Use for vinaigrettes, poultry and seafood marinades, seasoned crumbs, and butter blends.

Ingredients:
6 parts parsley
2 parts lemon rind
2 parts tarragon
1/4 part cloves
1/2 part bay leaves

SALSA HERB BLEND

Use in fresh salsas.

Ingredients:
4 parts parsley
1 part dried red pepper flakes
1 part dried onion flakes
1/2 part coriander seeds, crushed
1/2 part lime peel

CAJUN SPICE HERB BLEND

Use for meat rubs, marinades, butters, and crumb coatings.

Ingredients:
10 parts paprika
1 part cayenne pepper
1 part oregano
1 part sweet basil
1 part thyme
1 part cumin seeds
1 part garlic powder

CITRUS CINNAMON HERB BLEND

Use for poultry marinades, crumb toppings, spreads, fruit dips, and muffin mixes.

Ingredients:
3 parts brown sugar
1 part dried orange rind
1 part ground cinnamon
1/4 part allspice
1/4 part nutmeg

Making Herb Blends

RECIPES

HERBES DE PROVENCE

Use to season meats and for marinades, crumb mixtures, and butters.

Ingredients:
2 parts marjoram
2 parts oregano
1 part rosemary
1 part thyme
1/2 part lavender buds
1/2 part fennel seeds ∞

LEMON DILL HERB BLEND

This blend is our family favorite. It is excellent on roasted new potatoes and is also good in rice. Use it to create vinaigrettes, marinades, dips, and biscuit mixes.

Ingredients:
4 parts parsley
2 parts dill
1 part lemon granules
1 part garlic granules

CHIVE AND ONION HERB BLEND

Use for general seasoning, vinaigrettes, and dips.

Ingredients:
3 parts parsley
2 parts chives
1 part onion flakes
1 part garlic granules

GARDEN HERB BLEND

Use for vinaigrettes, dips, and biscuit mixes.

Ingredients:
3 parts parsley
1 part sage
1 part rosemary
1 part thyme
1/2 part garlic granules

HERBS AROMATIQUE BLEND

Use as a general seasoning—it makes an excellent salt substitute.

Ingredients:
4 parts parsley
2 parts garlic granules
1 part lovage
1 part pepper
1 part ground ginger
1 part paprika
1 part celery seeds
1 part onion powder
1 part basil

MEDITERRANEAN HERB BLEND

Use for vinaigrettes and dips.

Ingredients:
6 parts sundried tomatoes
3 parts basil
3 parts parsley
2 parts Greek oregano
1 part garlic granules
1 part lemon peel
1/2 part red pepper flakes

CHEESE AND HERB BLEND

Use for dips, spreads, and marinades.

Ingredients:
2 parts parsley
1 part onion flakes
1 part garlic granules
1 part buttermilk powder
1 part grated parmesan cheese
1/2 part lovage
1/4 part red pepper flakes
1/4 part celery seed

How to Use Herb Blends

These are some of my favorite recipes that use herb blends. Feel free to experiment with the blends to create your own gourmet dishes.

RECIPES

VINAIGRETTE
BASIC RECIPE

Mix:
1 tablespoon of herb blend (Lemon Dill, Garden Herb Blend, Mediterranean Blend, Lemon Clove, or Cheese and Herb)
1/4 cup olive oil
Juice of one lemon
1 tablespoon white wine vinegar
1 teaspoon sugar
Use:
Refrigerate for a few hours to allow the flavors to blend. Shake well before pouring. Great on salads as well as grilled vegetables.

MARINADE
BASIC RECIPE

Mix:
1 tablespoon herb blend (Lemon Clove, Citrus Cinnamon, Cajun Spice, Herbs de Provence, Herbs Aromatique, or Lemon Dill)
1/4 cup olive oil
1/4 cup water, orange juice, beer, or wine
Use:
Marinate meats or vegetables one hour or longer in this mix before grilling or roasting.

SALSA
BASIC RECIPE

Mix:
2 cups fresh tomatoes, finely chopped
1 cup red bell pepper, finely chopped
1 cup green pepper, finely chopped
1 red onion finely chopped
1 tablespoon Salsa Herb Blend
For a fruit salsa, add 1/2 cup chopped fresh mango, peach, or pineapple.
Use:
Refrigerate for 2 hours to allow the flavors to blend. Use with chips, on burritos and tacos, or on grilled fish and meats.

HERB CHEESE SPREAD
BASIC RECIPE

Mix:
1 tablespoon herb blend (Citrus Cinnamon, Herbs Aromatique, Chive and Onion, Garden Herb, or Cheese and Herb)
8 oz. soft cream cheese
Use:
Spread on bagels, English muffins, or crackers. *Serving option:* Form the mixture into small balls and roll in fresh chopped herbs. Serve with crackers for an attractive appetizer.

DIP BASIC RECIPE

Mix:
1 tablespoon herb blend (Lemon Dill, Chive and Onion, Garden Herb, or Mediterranean)
1 cup sour cream OR 1 cup thick yogurt
Use:
Serve with fresh or lightly steamed vegetables or with chips. This also is a wonderful topping for baked potatoes.

CRUMB COATING
BASIC RECIPE

Mix:
1 tablespoon herb blend (Lemon Clove, Cajun Spice, Herbs de Provence, Herbs Aromatique, Lemon Dill, or Garden Herb Blend)
2 cups dried bread crumbs
Use:
Use as a crumb coating for fish, poultry, or pork chops.

SAVORY TOPPING
BASIC RECIPE

Mix:
1 tablespoon butter
1 tablespoon herb blend (Lemon Clove, Cajun Spice, Herbs de Provence, Herbs Aromatique, Lemon Dill, or Garden Herb Blend)
2 cups dried bread crumbs
Use:
Sprinkle over casseroles before baking.

Making Fruit & Herb Butters

Flavored butters are a wonderful way to preserve fresh herbs for use all year round. Fruit butters make exceptional spreads for bagels, pancakes, or fresh rolls; savory herb blends are delightful on cooked vegetables, bread, and pasta. A corn roast becomes a gourmet feast when the corn is served with a selection of savory butters. Herb butters can be made with dried or fresh herbs.

R E C I P E S

DRIED HERB BUTTER BASIC RECIPE

Mix:
2 teaspoons dried herb blend
1/4 pound (1 stick) softened butter

Use:
Store in refrigerator. Use within one week.

FRESH HERB BUTTER BASIC RECIPE

Mix:
1/4 cup finely chopped herbs
1 pound (4 sticks) butter, room temperature

Use:
Place in an attractive crock or form into a cylinder, refrigerate, and slice. To make cylinders, place the butter on a piece of wax paper and roll into a cylinder. Wrap the cylinder with wax paper and twist the ends. Refrigerate until firm. Cylinders can be sliced for attractive display. To freeze, place the finished tubes in a large freezer bag. Fresh herb butters last for 3-4 months in your freezer or up to one week in the refrigerator. If you are planning to freeze fresh herb butters, use unsalted butter.

BERRY BUTTER

This is my sister Cathy's recipe. It's wonderful on freshly baked bread, warm croissants, or pancakes. This butter freezes well.

Ingredients:
1 cup fresh berries (We like strawberries best, but raspberries, cranberries, or blackberries also can be used.)
3/4 cup powdered sugar
1/4 pound butter
1/2 teaspoon vanilla (omit in cranberry butter and substitute 1/2 teaspoon fresh orange zest)

Here's How:
Wash and hull berries. Let berries dry completely. Cream together sugar and butter. Add vanilla and mix well. Gently fold in berries. Mix until well blended.

BASIL BUTTER

This is excellent on pasta or vegetables and in soups.

Ingredients:
1/4 cup fresh basil
1 garlic clove, minced fine
1 tablespoon fresh lemon juice
1 pound butter

Mix according to the basic recipe for Fresh Herb Butter.

GARDEN HERB BUTTER

Use on meats, fish, baked potatoes, and vegetables.

Ingredients:
2 tablespoons fresh tarragon
2 tablespoons chives
2 tablespoons parsley
1/2 teaspoon freshly ground pepper
1 pound butter

Mix according to the basic recipe for Fresh Herb Butter.

ORANGE AND GINGER BUTTER

For chicken, shellfish, or biscuits.

Ingredients:
2 tablespoons fresh orange zest
2 tablespoons grated fresh ginger root
1 tablespoon mint leaves
1 pound butter

Mix according to the basic recipe for Fresh Herb Butter.

FLOWER BUTTER RECIPES

Fresh flower petals can also be blended into flavorful butters.

Savory Nasturtium Butter: Slice nasturtium petals into long strips. Mix 1 tablespoon blossoms with 1/2 teaspoon freshly ground pepper. Add to 1/4 pound butter.

Sweet and Spicy Tea Party Butter: Mix 1 tablespoon each fresh anise hyssop, bee balm, and calendula blossoms with 1/4 pound butter.

Strawberry
Butter

Making Herbal & Fruit Vinegars

In the Victorian era, fresh herbs were used to create flavored vinegars. One turn-of-the-century cookbook had nearly 20 recipes for fruit, herbal, and floral blends. The spiced vinegar recipe was noted as a "nasal stimulant useful for reviving and refreshing those who suffer from faintness and nervous headaches." You can use herbal vinegars in salad dressings, vinaigrettes, and marinades or to deglaze a pan.

White, cider, and wine vinegars can all be flavored with herbs and fruits. Use large glass jars to "brew" your vinegars, then strain and decant in decorative jars or bottles. Use only non-metallic tops (glass, plastic, or cork).

For strong flavored vinegar, use lots of fresh herbs in your blends. I do not give exact measurements for these recipes—I measure by "handfuls" or "large bunches." I don't remove the leaves from the stems, but rather place the whole stem into the vinegar. The basic proportion is to fill a one gallon jar half full of fresh herbs, loosely packed, and fill the jar with vinegar.

▓ Basic Instructions for Herbal Vinegar

1. Gently heat the vinegar in a glass saucepan until it is very warm. Boiling the vinegar will harm the flavor and natural properties of the vinegar, but heating speeds the release of the flavors.
2. Place fresh herbs in a clean jar. Pour in warm vinegar to cover. Store in a dark, cool place for two weeks to allow the flavor to develop.
3. Decant the vinegar and strain through coffee filters. Pour into clean, decorative bottles.
4. Add a fresh herb sprig or recommended spices for an accent.

To store: Even though these vinegars look beautiful on a window ledge, they will last longer if kept in a dark area of the kitchen.

▓ Vinegar Variations

Fruit Vinegars: Warm 6 cups white wine vinegar. Dissolve 2 cups sugar in the vinegar. Add 3 cups fresh fruit (raspberries, blueberries, or cranberries). Follow the basic instructions for Herbal Vinegar.

Blossom Vinegars: Chive blossoms and nasturtiums make beautifully colored vinegars. Rose and lavender vinegars are useful personal fragrances and hair rinses. To make them, follow the basic instructions for Herbal Vinegar. *TIP:* The colors will be brighter if you don't heat the vinegar.

Single Blend Vinegars: Many single blend vinegars are popular, such as tarragon, raspberry, basil, and dill. Follow the basic instructions. ∾

ITALIAN VINEGAR RECIPE

Add to container:
Half fill a one-gallon jar with oregano, basil, and flat-leaf parsley.
Add:
2 fresh hot peppers
4 cloves garlic
Rind of one lemon
Use white vinegar and follow the basic instructions. Garnish bottles with a long strip of lemon zest, a clove of garlic, and oregano and parsley sprigs.

VICTORIAN SPICED VINEGAR RECIPE

Use this vinegar blend in coleslaw and potato salad.
Blend together and crush coarsely with a mortal and pestle:
1 tablespoon whole allspice
1 tablespoon celery seed
1 tablespoon whole cloves
1 tablespoon whole peppercorns
1 tablespoon whole mustard
Add:
2 tablespoons freshly grated ginger
3 cups sugar
Place in a one gallon jar. Fill with apple cider vinegar.
Complete according to basic instructions. ∾

TARRAGON SHALLOT VINEGAR RECIPE

In a gallon jar, place:
8 quartered shallots
Rind of one lemon
Fill the bottle half full with fresh tarragon and a handful of flat-leaf parsley. Use white wine vinegar and follow the basic instructions. Garnish the finished bottles with 1 finely chopped shallot, a few red and green peppercorns, and a sprig of fresh tarragon.

MINT SAUCE

This is the very best mint sauce recipe. It's wonderful on peas and small roasted potatoes and, of course, with lamb. It is a great way to preserve the fresh flavors of mint. Refrigerate this blend for up to one month.
Combine in a glass saucepan:
3/4 cup of strong, cold tea
1/4 cup sugar
Stir over medium heat until the sugar is dissolved.
Stir in:
1 cup freshly chopped mint
1/2 cup white vinegar
Use: Let stand 15 minutes before pouring into clean bottles. Shake before serving.

Additional recipes on page 62

HOT PEPPER VINEGAR

Italian Vinegar

Tarragon Shallot 6-8-98

Spiced Vinegar 15-7-98

Making Herbal & Fruit Vinegars

continued from page 60

LEMON VINEGAR RECIPE

In a gallon jar, place:
Rinds of two fresh lemons
1/4 cup white peppercorns
Fill the bottle with fresh lemon-scented herbs (lemon balm, lemon thyme, lemon scented geranium, lemon verbena). Use white wine vinegar and follow the basic instructions. Garnish the finished bottles with long strips of lemon zest and white peppercorns.

PEPPER VINEGAR RECIPE

This vinegar is hot and provides the kick for Mexican, Asian, and Creole dishes.
To a quart bottle of apple cider vinegar, add:
4 hot red chili peppers
1/4 cup mixed white, green, red, and black peppercorns
Follow the basic instructions. Garnish bottles with 1 tablespoon mixed peppercorns and a red chili pepper.

Making Herbal Oils

Herbal oils are very easy to make. They can be used in salad dressings and marinades, for stir-frying, and over hot pasta. Rosemary flavored oil and balsamic vinegar is remarkable for dipping crusty Italian or focaccia bread.

This section on flavored oils also includes recipes for dried tomatoes in oil and flavored cheese in herb oil, which can be served with crusty bread for a appetizing lunch.

■ Tips for Making Flavored Oils

- Use a good quality olive oil, sunflower oil, or canola oil.
- Finely chop the herbs and coarsely crush the spices for maximum flavor release.
- You may have read news reports concerning the danger of using garlic or onions in homemade oils. Because oils are not acidic, they are a perfect breeding ground for botulism. I think the possibility of poisoning someone with your gift outweighs having garlic or onion flavor, so I don't use garlic or onions in my recipes. You can, however, use a commercial garlic or onion concentrate in your flavored oils—usually a few drops is all you need.

■ Basic Instructions for Herbal Oils

1. Heat the oil gently until very warm.
2. Place the fresh herbs in a large glass bowl with a pouring spout. Cover them with warm oil.
3. Cover the bowl with plastic wrap. Let the flavors infuse the oil for 12 hours.
4. Strain the flavored oil through a fine strainer. Pour into clean, decorative bottles. Add a sprig of fresh herb to decorate.

To store: Store in a dark, cool place for up to 8 months. ∞

TOMATO AND ROSEMARY OIL RECIPE

Ingredients:
1/2 cup finely chopped dried tomatoes
1 cup extra virgin olive oil
2 cups sunflower oil
1/2 cup chopped fresh rosemary
Mix and bottle according to basic instructions. Decorate each bottle with a sprig of fresh rosemary.

OREGANO OIL RECIPE

Ingredients:
3 cups olive oil
1/2 cup chopped fresh oregano
1 teaspoon coarsely crushed peppercorns
2 bay leaves
Mix and bottle according to basic instructions. Decorate each bottle with a few whole peppercorns and a sprig of oregano.

HOT PEPPER OIL RECIPE

Ingredients:
2 cups canola oil
1/2 cup crushed dried red chili peppers
4 tablespoons mixed peppercorns, slightly crushed
Mix and bottle according to basic instructions. Decorate each bottle with one whole dried red chili pepper.

DRIED TOMATOES IN OIL

Fill a sterilized jar with sundried tomatoes, packing them loosely.
Combine in a saucepan:
1 teaspoon chopped dried oregano
1 teaspoon chopped dried parsley
1 teaspoon chopped dried basil
2/3 cup olive oil
Heat the oil and herbs gently until warm. Pour over the tomatoes. Store in the refrigerator. Use chopped dried tomatoes in oil to make pasta sauces and salad dressings, to flavor cream cheese, and on pizzas.

CHEESE IN HERBED OIL

Use feta cheese, baby mozzarella cheese (mozzarella di bufala), or fresh goat cheese (chevre) in this flavorful mix. *If using feta,* cover the cheese with 1 cup milk and 1 cup water. Let sit in the refrigerator overnight to remove the excess saltiness. Drain the cheese and pat dry.
Loosely pack the cheese in a 2 cup jar. Add:
3 sprigs fresh thyme
2 sprigs fresh rosemary
3 small fresh red chili peppers
1 tablespoon whole yellow mustard seeds
2 teaspoons fennel seed
4 bay leaves
Rind of one lemon
Pour over the top 2 cups olive oil, or enough to cover. Place in the refrigerator for one week before using to let the flavors develop. Keep in the refrigerator no longer than 3 months. ∾

Making Flavored Sugars

Flavored sugars are very simple and easy to create. These exotic sweeteners add subtle perfume and flavor to tea, fruit desserts, and baked goods. Use rose petals, mint leaves. scented geranium leaves, vanilla beans, or citrus peels for flavoring sugar.

▨ Basic Instructions

1. Layer the sugar and fresh petals, leaves, or peels in a glass jar. Cover tightly.
2. Place the covered jar in a dark place and let flavors develop for two to three weeks. Taste.
3. *Optional:* If you wish the sugar flavor to be stronger, repeat the process, using fresh petals, leaves, or peels.
4. After the sugar is flavored, pour into a bowl. Remove the petals, leaves, or peels. Strain the sugar through a fine sieve, if needed, to remove smaller pieces.

▨ Tips for Making Flavored Sugars

- Use superfine sugar (sometimes called "berry sugar").
- Let citrus rinds dry for a day before adding to the sugar.
- Slice open vanilla beans to release maximum flavor.
- To make colored sugar, place the flavored sugar in a large jar. Add a few drops of food coloring. Stir and shake well to evenly distribute the coloring. Use green for mint sugar, pink for rose sugar, orange for citrus sugar, etc. Layering colored flavored sugars in a jar is a charming presentation.
- Store flavored sugars in glass jars with tight-fitting lids. ∞

CITRUS CINNAMON SUGAR RECIPE

This is a refreshing sugar for tea and hot cereals. Keep in a wide-mouth jar.

Ingredients:
Superfine sugar
Lemon verbena leaves
Lemon rind
Orange peel
Cinnamon
Yellow food coloring
Orange food coloring
Whole cinnamon sticks
Dried orange peel stars

Here's How:
1. Make a batch of lemon flavored sugar by layering lemon verbena leaves and lemon rind. Color this batch a golden yellow.
2. Make a batch of orange and cinnamon flavored sugar. Mix sugar with 1 teaspoon cinnamon and layer with orange peel. Color this batch orange.
3. Layer the sugars in a jar, alternating with golden brown sugar. Push a few whole cinnamon sticks and dried orange stars into the sugar before placing the top on the jar.

VICTORIAN TEA SUGAR RECIPE

This sugar is pretty sprinkled on shortbread cookies or in a pound cake or a cup of tea.

Ingredients:
Superfine sugar
Rose petals
Rose scented geranium leaves
Vanilla beans
Red food coloring
Sugared flowers

Here's How:
1. Layer fresh rose petals, rose scented geranium leaves, and vanilla beans in the sugar.
2. After the sugar has been infused with the flavors, divide the batch into three separate jars.
3. Add one drop red food coloring to the first jar. Shake to blend.
4. Add three drops red food coloring to the second jar. Shake to blend.
5. Leave the third jar of sugar white. Layer the sugars in a pretty wide mouth jar.
6. Decorate the top of the sugar with sugared flowers.

Making Flavored Honey & Syrups

Flavored honey and syrups are sweet treats that are easy to make and a delight to give and use.

▨ Flavored Honey

Flavored honey is good in tea and in salad dressings, or mix it with an equal amount of butter to make a delicious spread for croissants, pancakes, muffins, and English muffins.

Use a light colored, liquid honey and fresh herbs to make flavored honey.

Here's How:
1. Mix 1 pint honey with 1 tablespoon fresh herbs in a glass saucepan. Heat gently in the microwave or in a double boiler until very warm. High heat will damage the honey. Let cool.
2. Decant the honey into a large jar with a tight-fitting lid. Let the honey steep four to five days in a cool, dark place.
3. Gently reheat the honey and strain through a fine sieve.
4. Bottle the flavored honey in sterilized jars.
5. Add some finely chopped herbs or flowers, citrus zest, or spices to decorate the jars.

To store: Store flavored honey in a dark, cool area. It will last indefinitely. ∾

▨ Fruit Syrups

Fruit syrups are made by adding enough sugar to ripe fruit to preserve them. Choose fresh, fully ripe fruit with no blemishes for peak flavor.

Fruit syrups are delicious as a drink mixed with sparkling water, or use them full strength to top pancakes, custards, or ice cream. Syrups also can be used to decorate dessert plates (as is done in fine restaurants).

The simplest way to make syrups is in the microwave. If you do not have a microwave, gently cook the mixture in a double boiler until heated. (Using a double boiler lessens the chance of burning the mix.) You can use fresh or frozen fruit.

continued on page 68

FRUITS FOR CREATING SYRUPS

Raspberries
Blackberries (Add 10 whole allspice, 1 stick of cinnamon and 6 whole cloves, all slightly crushed, to the mixture for a ambrosial, spicy blend.)
Blueberries
Strawberries
Purple plums
Red currants

RECIPES

ROSEMARY AND ORANGE HONEY

Ingredients:
2 teaspoons fresh rosemary leaves
1 tablespoon orange zest
1 pint honey
Optional: 1 teaspoon Grand Marnier liqueur
Prepare according to basic instructions. Decorate the jar with orange zest.

CLOVE AND GINGER HONEY

Ingredients:
1 teaspoon whole cloves
1 tablespoon chopped candied ginger
1 pint honey
Prepare according to basic instructions. Decorate the jar with a piece of candied ginger studded with 3 whole cloves.

MINT HONEY

Ingredients:
1 tablespoon freshly chopped mint
1 pint honey
Prepare according to basic instructions.

FLORAL HONEY

Ingredients:
1 tablespoon fresh rose petals or rose scented geranium leaves
1 teaspoon lavender buds
1 pint honey
Prepare according to basic instructions. Decorate the jar with a few dried miniature rosebuds.

HERB HONEY

Ingredients:
1 teaspoon lemon thyme
1 teaspoon tarragon
1 teaspoon sage
1 pint honey
Prepare according to basic instructions.

Making Flavored Honey & Syrups

Fruit Syrups (cont.)

Ingredients:

2 cups fresh ripe berries
1 cup sugar
3/4 cup light corn syrup

Here's How:

1. Place fruit in a glass bowl and cover with plastic wrap. Heat in the microwave on high for 10 minutes or until boiling, stirring every 3 minutes.
2. Line a strainer with cheesecloth and place over a bowl. Pour the hot fruit into the lined strainer. Press with a wooden spoon to remove the juice. Discard the pulp.
3. Add the sugar and corn syrup to the fruit juices. Heat until the mixture comes to a boil, stirring every 2 minutes. Boil for a full minute.
4. Skim off any foam from the top. Pour the hot syrup into sterilized jars.

To store: Refrigerate no longer than 6 months.

Use: To make a fruit drink, place 2 tablespoons syrup in an 8 oz. glass. Top with sparkling water. Add ice cubes. Adjust the ratio to your own taste. ∾

Old Fashioned Lemonade Syrup

This recipe has been in my husband's family for years. It is very close to the lemon syrup recipe in my 1894 cookbook!

Ingredients:

1 cup lemon juice (The juice of 6 lemons equals 1 cup.)
4 cups sugar
4 cups boiling water
2-3/4 tablespoons citric acid
2-1/4 teaspoons tartaric acid
1 teaspoon epsom salts
Grated rinds of two lemons

Mix the ingredients well to dissolve the sugar. Refrigerate. Use to make lemonade, mixing with water and ice cubes.

Making Flavored Teas

I have never been a great fan of herbal teas, but I enjoy these flavored blends of tea and dried herbs. They give me gentle scents and aromas of herbs along with the satisfying comfort of a hot cup of orange pekoe. For iced tea, double amounts of the herbs and tea to make a strong brew before pouring over ice cubes.

For giving, simply blend dried herbs with loose tea and package. The recipes given will make one 6 cup pot of tea. ∾

Luscious Lemon Tea Recipe

Ingredients:

1 teaspoon dried lemon verbena
1 teaspoon lemon grass
1/2 teaspoon dried minced lemon peel
3 tablespoons orange pekoe tea

Lovely Lavender Tea Recipe

Ingredients:

1/2 teaspoon dried lavender buds
1 teaspoon dried rose petals
4 tablespoons orange pekoe tea

Spicy Rose Tea Recipe

Ingredients:

4 tablespoons orange pekoe tea
1 teaspoon dried rose geranium leaves
Cinnamon stick, 1" long, broken into small pieces.

My Favorite Blend Tea Recipe

Ingredients:

1 teaspoon dried peppermint leaves
1 teaspoon lemon verbena
1 teaspoon rose hips
1 teaspoon hibiscus flowers
3 tablespoons orange pekoe tea

Herbs Suitable for Making Teas

Anise hyssop
Bee balm
Chamomile
Lavender
Lemon hyssop
Lemon verbena
Lemon balm
Lemon thyme
Mint
Mints
Rose petals
Rosemary
Sage
Scented geraniums
Thyme

Making Spirited Fruits & Liquors

Spirited fruits are a wonderful idea for preserving the fresh fruits of summer for elegant gift giving during the holiday season. Liquors and flavored vodkas are also very easy to make.

I first learned about preserving fruits in spirits when I watched my Grandfather Laturnus fill jars with ripe cherries and sugar and pour vodka to cover. A curious child, I really wanted a taste, so Grandpa let me try them one day. (My mother disapproved—it was, after all, breakfast.) Not surprisingly, I hated the taste, although I have come to appreciate the rich tastes of spirited fruits spooned over pound cake, custard, or ice cream.

When I asked my aunts for Grandpa's recipe, it was simple: Pour brandy, rum, or vodka over sugar and summer ripened fruit, and let sit until Christmas time.

Spirited Fruits

In France, they use brandy; in Germany, they use rum. Your choice!

Use These Fruits:
Blueberries, raspberries, blackberries, strawberries, and currants
Grapes and cherries
Peaches and apricots, peeled and cut into pieces
Plums, peeled and cut in half
Do not use: apples, pears, or bananas.

Here's How:
1. Sterilize a large decorative jar with boiling water.
2. Place several inches of fruit in the jar. Pour in sugar to cover the fruit. A basic ratio is 2 cups fruit to 1/2 cup sugar.
3. Pour in enough rum or brandy to completely cover the fruit.
4. Cover the jar. Store in the refrigerator. Add additional layers of fruit to the jar as the fruit comes into season. Jars of single fruits also can be created, such as brandied peaches or cherries in vodka. Let stand several months before using. ∾

Flavored Vodkas

Flavored vodkas are used to make unusual spiced drinks. They are super simple to create—just place the fruit, spice, or herb in a decorative bottle and add vodka. Let the flavors saturate the vodka for about three months before decanting, straining, and using. These bottled spirits are beautiful to display in the kitchen as the vodka infuses with flavors. ∾

RECIPES

BLACKBERRY BRANDY

Ingredients:
1 quart fresh blackberries
3/4 cup sugar
3/4 teaspoon whole allspice
12 whole cloves
2 cups brandy

In a gallon jar with a tight-fitting, screw-top lid, combine berries, sugar, and spices. Pour in the brandy and store in the refrigerator. Every once in a while, invert the jar to mix. After two months, strain the mixture through a cheesecloth-lined strainer, pressing the juice with the back of a wooden spoon. Discard the pulp.

FIREWORKS VODKA

This makes one fiery caesar!
Place in 1 pint vodka:
2 fresh red chili peppers, cut in half

CITRUS VODKA

Ingredients:

1 orange	1 lemon	1 lime

Cut the fruit into 1/4" slices.
Place in a wide-mouth quart jar. Add vodka to cover.

SPICED VODKA

Place in 1 pint vodka:
1 tablespoon allspice berries
3 cinnamon sticks
1 teaspoon whole cloves

HERB VODKA

Ingredients:

Dill	Lovage
Sage	Thyme

Rind of one lemon
Place a handful of each herb plus the lemon rind in a quart jar. Cover with vodka.

Making Biscuit & Muffin Mixes

Quick bread mixes are easy to make—simply combine the dry ingredients and package. Add instructions that tell how to add fresh, wet ingredients and bake. You can package your favorite cookie, biscuit, scone, or quick bread recipes in this manner for giving. Layering the dry ingredients in a clear cellophane bag makes an inviting package. I have seen these mixes in stores for over $6! You can create your own for much less money.

▓ Biscuit or Scone Mixes

Ingredients:
3 cups whole wheat flour
3 cups all purpose flour
2 cups powdered buttermilk
3 tablespoons baking powder
2 teaspoons salt
1 cup shortening

Here's How:
In a large bowl, sift together all the dry ingredients. With two knives or a pastry cutter, cut in the shortening until the mixture resembles fine crumbs. Refrigerate this mixture for up to two weeks or freeze up to three months. Makes 10 cups biscuit mix.

To Bake:
Pour 2 cups of bisquit mix into a bowl. Add 1 large egg, lightly beaten, and 1/3 cup milk. Stir until mixture forms a ball. Do not over mix. Turn out the dough on a lightly floured surface and pat out to 3/4" thickness. Cut the dough into 10 pieces of equal size. Arrange 2" apart on an ungreased baking sheet. Bake in a 450 degree F. oven for 10 to 12 minutes until lightly browned.

Cheese and Sage Biscuits:
Combine 2 cups biscuit mix with 1/2 cup parmesan cheese, 2 tablespoons dried sage, and 1 tablespoon dried parsley. Package with instructions for baking.

Garden Herb Biscuits:
Combine 2 cups biscuit mix with 1 tablespoon of the Garden Herb Blend. (See the Herb Blends section for recipe.) Package with instructions for baking.

Lemon Dill Biscuits:
Combine 2 cups biscuit mix with 1 tablespoon Lemon Dill Herb Blend. (See the Herb Blends section for recipe.) Package with instructions for baking.

Cranberry Scones:
Combine 2 cups biscuit mix with 3 tablespoons brown sugar, 1 tablespoon dried cranberries, and 1 teaspoon dried orange zest. Package with instructions for baking. Substitute light cream for milk in the baking instructions.

Candied Ginger Scones
Combine 2 cups biscuit mix with 3 tablespoons brown sugar and 1 tablespoon chopped candied ginger. Package with instructions for baking. Substitute light cream for milk in the baking instructions.

For Gift Giving:
Put 2 cups biscuit mix in each package. One package will make 10 biscuits. Include the following instructions with biscuit or scone mixes:
Basic Biscuit or Scone Recipe
Pour the contents of this package into a bowl. Add 1 large egg, lightly beaten, and 1/3 cup milk. Stir until mixture forms a ball. Do not over mix. Turn out the dough on a lightly floured surface and pat out to 3/4" thickness. Cut the dough into 10 pieces of equal size. Arrange 2" apart on an ungreased baking sheet. Bake in a 450 degree F. oven for 10 to 12 minutes until lightly browned. ∽

▓ Muffin Mixes

Ingredients:
5 cups sugar
12 cups all purpose flour
4 tablespoons baking powder
1 tablespoon salt
2 cups shortening

Here's How:
In a large bowl, sift together the dry ingredients. With two knives or a pastry cutter, cut in the shortening until the mixture resembles fine crumbs. Refrigerate this mixture for up to two weeks or freeze up to three months. Makes 20 cups muffin mix.

To Bake:
Pour 4 cups of mix in a large bowl. Add 2 eggs, lightly beaten, and 1 cup milk. Stir until mixture is just moistened. Fill paper-lined or greased muffin cups 2/3 full. Bake in a 400 degree F. oven for 20-25 minutes or until done.

Pecan Cranberry Muffins:
Combine 4 cups muffin mix with 1/2 cup broken pecans, 1/2 cup dried cranberries, and 1 teaspoon dried lemon granules. Package with instructions for baking.

Citrus Cinnamon Muffins:
Combine 4 cups muffin mix with 1 tablespoon of Citrus Cinnamon Blend. (See Herb Blends section for recipe.) Package with instructions for baking.

Oatmeal Fruit Muffins:
Combine 4 cups muffin mix with 1/4 cup regular rolled oats, 1 teaspoon powdered cinnamon, 1/2 cup golden raisins, 1/2 cup dried apricots, 1/4 cup chopped dates, and 1 teaspoon dried orange granules. Package with instructions for baking.

For Gift-Giving:
Put 4 cups muffin mix in each package. Each package will make a dozen large muffins. Include the following instructions with muffin mixes:
Pour the contents of this package in a large bowl. Add 2 eggs, lightly beaten, and 1 cup milk. Stir until mixture is just moistened. Fill paper-lined or greased muffin cups 2/3 full. Bake in a 400 degree F. oven for 20-25 minutes or until done. ∽

PRESSED FLOWER PRETTIES

Brightly colored, perfectly preserved pressed flowers are wonderful for creating two-dimensional projects. Use them on candles, soaps, jars, and pots, under glass, and for cards and paper sachets.

Waxing Pressed Flowers
on
Candles & Soaps

Pressed blossoms imbedded on pillar and tapered candles make elegant hostess gifts, and they are a beautiful addition to a gift basket. The same technique is used for decorating soaps. The flowers last as long as the soap!

There are two techniques for waxing flowers on candles and one for soaps, the immersion technique and the dipped technique. Use the immersion technique for tapers and large pillar candles. Either technique can be used on votives and short pillar candles. Use the dipped technique only for soaps. ∾

Pictured at right: Candles and soaps, decorated with pressed flowers and leaves, and pansy petals pressed under glass. See pages 76 & 77 for instructions.

Making Floral Candles & Soaps

▦ Floral Candles—Immersion Technique

You Will Need:

A selection of pressed flowers

A white short pillar, short taper, or votive candle (smaller candles are easier to work with)

Paraffin wax

A container deep enough to accommodate enough paraffin to completely submerge the candle (I use a large, clean tin.)

A water bath (an electric skillet or large pan to fill with water and hold the tin)

Small, soft paint brush

Candle holder (If you're working with tapers)

Old nylon stocking

Wax paper

Here's How:

1. Experiment with the flowers to get an idea of how you are going to place them on the candle. Once you start, you will need to work quickly, so be ready.

2. To find out how much paraffin you need, do the following exercise before starting: Place your candle in the tin and pour in water until it covers the candle. (You will need to hold down the candle—it will want to float to the top.) Take out the candle and mark the water level on the outside of the tin with a permanent marker. Pour the water out and dry the candle and the tin. Melt wax in the tin until it reaches the mark. Keep the wax in the water bath to keep it liquid.

3. With the paint brush, paint a little wax on the candle where you wish to place the first flower. Gently press the flower on the wax. Repeat with the remaining blossoms and/or leaves.

4. When you are satisfied with the placement, dip the entire candle into the wax. Hold by the wick. Use a smooth motion when dipping, and do not hesitate during the dip. Only dip the candle once. CAUTION: wax is hot. Do not put fingers in wax. Lift the candle out of the wax and place it in a candle holder (if a taper) or on a piece of wax paper.

5. Let the wax shell cool and harden over the blossoms. (It will look cloudy when it first comes out but will dry clear.)

6. Buff the finished candle with a piece of soft nylon stocking for a shiny finish. ∾

▦ Floral Candles—Dipped Technique

You Will Need:

A selection of pressed flowers

A white short pillar or votive candle (smaller candles are easier to work with)

Paraffin wax

Water bath (an electric skillet or large pan)

A low pan to hold the wax, such as a foil tin

Small, soft paint brush

Old nylon stocking

DIPPED TECHNIQUE

1. Applying melted wax to the side of a candle with a paint brush.

2. Gently pressing the flowers in the wax.

3. Dipping the candle to seal the flowers with melted paraffin.

Here's How:

1. Experiment with the flowers to get an idea of how you are going to place them on the candle. Once you start, you will need to work quickly, so be ready.
2. Melt paraffin wax in the foil pan in an electric skillet or pan filled with 1" of water on the stove. Keep the wax in the water bath to keep it liquid.
3. With the paint brush, paint a little wax on the candle where you wish to place the first flower **(photo 1)**. Gently press the flower on the wax **(photo 2)**. Repeat with the remaining blossoms and/or leaves.
4. When you are satisfied with the placement, hold the candle at each end and dip and roll the side of candle in the wax **(photo 3)**. Use a smooth motion when dipping, and do not hesitate during the dip. Lift the candle out of the wax. Make sure the blossoms are completely covered and there are no air bubbles. If not, dip again. CAUTION: wax is hot. Do not put fingers in wax.
5. Let the wax shell cool and harden over the blossoms. (It will look cloudy when it first comes out but will dry clear.)
6. Buff the finished candle with a piece of soft nylon stocking for a shiny finish. ∽

Floral Soap

Use the dipped technique for making floral soap.

You Will Need:

Smooth bar of soap with a flat surface
Selection of pressed flowers
Electric skillet or large pan filled with water
Paraffin wax in a low container (I use a foil pan.)
Small, soft paint brush
Old nylon stocking

Here's How:

1. Decide how you wish to arrange the blossoms on one side of the soap.
2. Melt paraffin wax in the foil pan in an electric skillet or pan filled with 1" of water on the stove. Keep the wax in the water bath to keep it liquid.
3. With the paint brush, paint a little wax on the soap where you wish to place the first flower. Gently press the flower on the wax. Repeat with the remaining blossoms and/or leaves.
4. Dip the blossom side of the soap into the melted wax with a smooth motion and bring it up evenly. Make sure the blossoms are completely covered and there are no air bubbles. Dip once more if needed. Dip only one side of the soap, or you will completely seal it and it won't be usable.
5. Let cool. Buff the cooled and hardened soap with a nylon stocking. ∽

Beeswax Balloon Candle

This dipped candle shell is easy to make. It will hold a votive candle, and when the candle is lit, you can see the silhouettes the pressed flowers and foliage.

You Will Need:

Beeswax   A balloon
Dried pressed flowers and foliage
Wide-mouth container for heating wax
Water bath (electric skillet or large pan)
Foil tin
Optional: candle thermometer

Here's How:

1. Fill a balloon with water to the size shell desired. Tie the top of the balloon with string. Make sure the balloon fits easily in the wide-mouth container with room to spare.
2. Melt the beeswax in the wide-mouth container in a water bath. Have the pressed foliage with which you wish to decorate the candle shell ready.
3. After the wax has melted, keep it liquid and at a constant temperature in a water bath. If you have a candle thermometer, the perfect temperature for dipping is 160 degrees F.
4. Dip the balloon into the wax about halfway up and remove. Continue to dip the balloon, allowing it to cool slightly in between each dipping, until the shell is about 1/4" thick.
5. When you are near the end of the dipping, press dried flowers into the soft wax and dip a few more times.
6. Lift the shell from the wax. Hang it to dry with the string tied to the top of the balloon. (You may need someone to help at this stage.) Let cool.
7. Over a sink, break the balloon, pour out the water, and remove it.
8. To make a flat bottom, place a foil tin in the water bath and heat. Rub the bottom of the wax shell over the foil plate to melt the bottom flat. Use the same technique to even out and smooth the top.
9. Place a tea light or votive candle inside, light it, and admire the beautiful glow. ∽

Decoupaged Pressed Flowers

My early experiences with decoupaging my pressed flowers weren't as successful as I'd wished—the blossoms are very fragile, and working with them on hard or curved surfaces was difficult. Decoupaging also can re-introduce moisture to the blossoms, and the added moisture turns some flowers brown. I found I got the best results using a waterbase acrylic decoupage medium and applying a very thin coat for the first layer to seal the blossoms. I found that I could decoupage some dried flowers more successfully than others; it's a good idea to experiment so you'll know which blossoms hold up.

My frustration led me to develop an alternative technique that works very well and is very easy to do. I discovered that color photocopies of pressed flowers were virtually impossible to distinguish from real pressed flowers after decoupaging. Using color photocopies of pressed flowers makes it very easy to create projects, even for beginners.

Decoupaging with Photocopied Dried Flowers

This method works well on a variety of surfaces. Using photocopies, you can successfully add faux finishes such as crackle or antiquing after decoupaging without damaging the pressed flowers.

Create master sheets for copying by arranging the blossoms on a piece of paper. Group the blossoms into tiny arrangements as well as placing single blossoms on the sheet. Try to fill up the whole sheet. Make several sheets using different colored backgrounds. Use tiny amounts of craft glue—just enough to hold the blossoms in place—and carefully cover with a clear matte laminating sheet. After you've made your photocopies, you're ready to decoupage.

You Will Need:
Color photocopies of pressed flowers and leaves
Acrylic decoupage medium, the type that works as both a glue and a varnish
A surface (painted clay pots, wooden objects (sealed or painted), blank journals, or card stock)
Large, flat paint brush
Pair of small, sharp scissors

Here's How:
1. Choose a sheet of photocopied blossoms with a background color close to the color of your surface—that way, you won't have to cut out all the fine details. When the background is the same color as the surface, the paper outline is hard to detect. (This works best on light, rather than dark, backgrounds.)
2. Cut the photocopied blossoms from the sheet with scissors.
3. On a protected surface, coat the back of the cutout with a even layer of decoupage medium. Make sure to coat the entire surface.
4. Place the cutout motif on your project. Smooth it with your fingers to remove any wrinkles or air bubbles. Let dry.
5. Add two to three coats of decoupage medium. Allow the medium to dry between coats. ∽

Decoupaged Terra Cotta Saucer

A large terra cotta saucer decoupaged with pressed flowers makes a lovely gift container. A smaller saucer could be used for a soap dish.

You Will Need:
A terra cotta saucer
White acrylic craft paint
Photocopies of dried pressed flowers on a white background
Waterbase decoupage medium
Waterbase crackle medium
Waterbase varnish
Dark brown antiquing gel
4 wooden beads
Glue gun and glue sticks
Sponge brushes or bristle paint brushes
Small, sharp scissors

Here's How:
1. Paint the inside of the saucer with white paint. Let dry.
2. Cut out the flowers and position them. Glue to surface with decoupage medium. Let dry.
3. Apply two to three additional coats decoupage medium. Let dry between coats. Let final coat dry.
4. Apply waterbase crackle medium according to package instructions. Let dry.
5. Brush waterbase varnish over the crackle medium to make the cracks appear. Let dry.
6. Rub the crackled area with dark brown antiquing gel to highlight the crackled design. Let dry.
7. Glue the wooden beads to the bottom of the saucer for "feet." ∽

Making Labels & Cards

Use the photocopy method to create labels and card designs. Create sheets of pressed flower designs, photocopy, and cut out; then adhere the paper to card stock with a glue stick or spray adhesive.

You can create "moisten and stick" stickers, stamps, labels, and book plates by painting the backs of the photocopies with 1 part craft glue and 1/2 part white vinegar. Apply two coats. Let dry between coats. ∽

Recline and Relax
Bath Herb Blend

Pressed Flowers Under Glass

Pressed flowers are beautiful and durable under glass. Use these techniques to create frames, pictures, and coasters. The flowers are sandwiched between pieces of glass or mat board and glass and sealed on the edges with adhesive-backed copper foil tape.

Use rectangular or square pieces of glass 1/8" thick to cover your pressed flower arrangement. For each project, you'll need two pieces of glass or one piece of glass and a piece of mat board (available at frame shops and art supply stores) cut to the same size. You can have a glazier cut the glass for you or you can cut it yourself.

Shops that carry supplies for making stained glass sell copper foil tape as well as all sorts of beveled glass pieces and fancy textured and colored glass that can enhance your floral designs.

Arrange pressed flowers on the matboard.

Seal edges with copper foil tape.

Basic Pressing Under Glass Instructions

You Will Need:

2 pieces of glass cut the same size OR 1 piece of glass and 1 piece of mat board cut the same size
A selection of pressed flowers   Copper foil tape, 1/2" wide   White craft glue
Small paint brush   Large binder clips

Here's How:

1. Clean the glass pieces. Handle them by the edges after cleaning to prevent fingerprints, and be careful not to cut yourself.
2. Arrange the pressed flowers on one piece of glass or the mat board piece, using tiny amounts of craft glue to hold the flowers in place. Let the glue dry completely before proceeding.
3. Carefully place a piece of glass on top, sandwiching the flowers. Use binder clips to hold the pieces in place.
4. Measure the circumference of the piece and add 1/2". Cut a piece of copper foil tape to that measurement. Carefully peel back about 3" of the protective paper backing and center the tape on the edge. Remove the clips and protective paper as you go around the edges. As you complete each side, fold the edges of the tape over to the front and back.
5. With your fingernail, burnish the copper tape firmly.

Floral Coasters: To make a practical, pretty coaster, cut two pieces of glass 4" square.

Framed Collage: Arrange a photograph or a collage of photos on one piece of glass. If you like, add ticket stubs, pieces of lace, letters, or other memorabilia. Arrange pressed flowers around the photos. Use very little glue to help hold everything in place. Top with a second piece of glass and secure the edges with tape. Display the finished collage on a small easel or on a shelf with a plate rail. You can also create your collage on a piece of mat board and top with a piece of glass cut to the same dimensions.

Pressed Flower Pictures for Hanging: Keep these arrangements small so they are not too heavy to hang. A good size is 3" x 5". Make a decorative hanger with 19 gauge black wire by cutting an 8" piece of wire and curling the ends. Bend the wire so that it rests on top of the finished glass picture. Glue the wire hanger to the picture with a strong jewelry glue. Let the glue dry completely. Use small pieces of copper tape where the hanger meets the picture for extra strength.

Refrigerator Magnets: Make floral magnets to use on your refrigerator or filing cabinet. For each, use a 2-1/2" square of glass and a piece of mat board the same size. Apply a 2" piece of self-adhesive magnet stripping on the back. ∽

Making Decorated Paper Envelopes & Packages

Pressed flowers can be used to make laminated paper for packaging. Use the laminated paper to create decorative envelopes or bags: transfer the pattern, cut out, fold, and glue. Envelopes can be used as drawer sachets by placing your favorite fragrant sachet blend inside and sealing with glue.

You Will Need:

Pressed flowers   Plastic coated freezer paper   Sheer rice paper   An iron

Here's How:

1. Place the freezer paper, shiny side up, on an ironing board. Arrange pressed flowers on the paper. Cover with a sheet of sheer rice paper.
2. With a medium hot iron, press the paper to fuse the rice paper to the freezer paper, sandwiching the pressed flowers between them. ∽

DRIED FLOWER DECORATIONS

In this section are techniques for creating professional, beautiful, and unique dried flower arrangements and ornaments. Nature has done most of the work for you, creating gorgeous colors, textures, and forms in the dried flowers—you simply need to assemble them. Using dried flowers rather than artificial ones enables you to create with a permanent piece of your garden. The cost of the artificial flowers can be enormous, up to $100 in supplies for a large arrangement. Even though a dried arrangement will last two to three years, you can afford to create a new one each summer from blossoms preserved from your garden. The tools and materials needed to create with dried flowers are few and simple.

How to Use Dried Flowers

◼ Some Tips for Creating Dried Floral Designs

The first rule is there are no rules. However, beginners may find these tips useful.

- Many of the best designers have no formal training in floral design. They tend to work "outside the box," which makes their designs exciting and new.
- Design with the flowers you have on hand. If the design looks good to you, then it is perfect.
- Consider the environment your arrangement will live in. Will it sit on a table or hang on a wall? Make sure you design your piece from the perspective in which it will be seen.
- Think about what will be around your arrangement. Be sure the colors, textures, and general style fit the room. You will not want a light, country design in a den decorated in a dark, formal style.
- Use nature as inspiration. Plants naturally grow in interesting designs and are always well proportioned. Studying natural forms help you make the right decisions when designing.
- Use a variety of shapes, textures, and colors to make the design interesting. Have large flowers, long and thin branches of small buds, and airy, small flowers for filler.
- Design within the limits of the plant. For example, strong stemmed wheat cannot hang down gracefully from a vase—it grows straight and tall. Choose a design that fits the plant's natural shape.
- Keep the overall shape in mind. If you want to create a cone-shaped arrangement, keep to that shape as you plan and place the materials.
- Design with a focal point (a place where the eye naturally goes). For example, if you place a large silica dried rose at the corner of a frame, all the other plant materials should relate to this focal point.
- When choosing colors of dried material to use in your arrangement, remember that nothing in nature clashes. (An arrangement can, however, clash with its surround-

ings.) Using one color of dried flowers (for example, a variety of shades of purple) can make a dramatic arrangement, but so can arrangements with several colors.
- Use green in your arrangements. It shows off all the other colors, and it is the base color of nature.
- Bows are not the only accent for a dried arrangement—try objects such as a ceramic cherub, a mushroom, a bird, a small stuffed teddy bear, or a piece of lace. Choose objects that are simple, with one overall color, or they will get lost.
- Use a glue gun or thick white craft glue to attach the dried florals.
- If you have studied floral design, you will note that I work "backwards." Many designers start with the filler to create the general outline of the design, then add secondary plant materials, and finish with the large focal points. I arrange in the opposite order. I taught dried floral arranging at my store for seven years, and no one left a class without a sensational arrangement using my technique. However, another teacher taught using the method that starts with the filler, and her students created beautiful designs as well. Use the method that suits you.

◼ Arrangements with a Moss Base

Some interesting designs I have created with dried flowers have been arranged not in vases or on wreaths, but on basket handles, in open books, on bird cages, and other unlikely surfaces. This technique is done by draping a mixture of glue and Spanish moss on the object to create the base. The moss base raises the area where the design will be built, so it highlights the design. It's also natural looking—unlike floral foam, you don't need to hide it. The flowers are glued to this base, and the arrangement created.

When deciding on a surface for creating your design, look for interesting objects at tag sales or choose a piece you already own and give it new life. You might choose an old bird cage or a small, pretty spoon. Don't use valuable or precious objects that can't be replaced—use something that you

continued on page 84

How to Use Dried Flowers

Arrnagements with a Moss Base (cont.)

don't mind getting glue all over. This is a very messy technique, so make sure your work area is protected.

Take some time to plan your design. Sketching it roughly on a piece of paper can help you decide what flowers to use.

You Will Need:
A surface
Spanish Moss
White craft glue
Dried flowers
Optional: Glue gun and glue sticks

Here's How:
1. Take a large handful of Spanish moss. Pour about 1/4 cup white glue on it. Pick up the moss and mix the glue into it by pulling the moss apart. (You want the strands of the moss to be coated in the glue.) Don't mash the moss into a tight wad—you want it to be light and airy. Don't worry, the glue will dry clear. Don't run to the sink to wash off your hands—you'll find it's easier to rub your hands free of the moss and glue. When most of the mess is off your hands, take off the rest at the sink.
2. Drape the glue-saturated moss over your object according to your design plan. The dried flowers will be glued to this base. *Tip:* If you have any glue-saturated moss left, form a small bird's nest with it to use in a future arrangement. Let dry.
3. Pull on the moss to make sure it is firmly attached to your object. If there are any weak spots, secure them with a glue gun.
4. Place the large items first. (These could be large flowers for the focal point or accents like a birdhouse.)
5. Arrange the remaining materials to accent and embellish the large objects.
6. Finish off the design with a filler such as baby's breath, statice, or another light, airy dried material. ∽

Fairy Basket

This arrangement was created using the glue and moss method. The moss base was wrapped and draped around the handle. When dry, the small flowers were glued individually to the base. Arrange one type of plant material on the base at a time to make sure the material is evenly distributed. Silver bouillon was draped through the finished design to give the basket a magical appearance. Display your finished basket in a special spot and you may have a fairy or two come and visit. ∽

Dried Flower Decorated Hat

For this hat, I formed a wire wreath base on which I affixed small bundles of dried flowers. The wire base allowed me to design several interchangeable wreaths that can be put on the hat to match the occasion and the color of my dress. (The wreath also can be worn on your head without a hat.)

You Will Need:
A hat
22 gauge covered stem wire
Florist's tape
Dried flowers (I used miniature pink roses, larkspur, small white strawflowers, lavender, and a green filler.)
Thin craft wire on a spool
Optional: Ribbon to make a bow

Here's How:
1. Measure the hat around the base of the crown and add 2". Cut a piece of 22 gauge stem wire to that length. If needed, use florist's tape to join two pieces of wire to make a piece that's long enough.
2. Form a circle with the wire. Bend one end of the wire into a loop and the other end into a hook to secure. Try the wreath form on the hat and adjust as needed.
3. Cut the plant material into sprigs 5-6" long. Create small bundles of flowers, wrapping the stems with thin craft wire. You will need 10-11 bundles for a medium-size hat.
4. Using a continuous piece of thin craft wire, attach the bundles to the wire base. Continue until the wire base is completely covered with flowers.
5. Adjust the wreath, if needed, so that the wreath fits snugly around the crown of the hat.
6. *Option:* Make a bow from ribbon and attach at the back of the wreath with wire.

To store: If you remove the wreath from the hat, hang the floral wreath from a dresser mirror or a peg to accent a room. You also can hang the hat on the wall when you're not wearing it. ∽

Dried Fruits & Seed Pods

Arranging with whole dried fruits and seed pods offers design challenges. After fruits and seed pods have dried, they need strong stems to push into floral foam. Use this technique to add stems to dried fruits, seed pods, and nuts.

You Will Need:
Whole dried fruits, dried seed pods, or nuts
An awl
White craft glue
Bamboo skewers of various lengths
Optional: Drill and small drill bit

Here's How:
1. At the bottom of the fruit, pod, or nut make a small hole with an awl. If the item is too hard, use a drill fitted with a small bit. (I rarely have to use a drill, as the awl is quite effective in making holes in even the hardest of shells.)
2. Choose a bamboo skewer of a length that will work for your arrangement. Dip the end of the skewer in a jar of white craft glue. Push the glue-dipped skewer in the hole you made. Let dry.

Option: Simply push the skewer into the fresh fruit before drying. As the fruit dries and shrinks, it will hold the stem firmly in place. ✍

Della Robbia Arrangement

You Will Need:
A container
Floral foam (Be sure to buy floral foam designed for dried flowers and wired material. The kind I use is called "Sahara"; the floral foam for fresh flowers is called "Oasis."
Glue gun and glue sticks
Floral anchor
Dried botanicals (fruits, nuts, pods, artificial grapes, rose heads)
Metallic gold filler
Wire pins

Here's How:
1. For the base, carve floral foam into a cone shape.
2. Glue a floral anchor to the bottom of the pot to hold the foam firmly in place. Place the foam in the pot.
3. Arrange fruits, nuts, pods, artificial grapes, and rose heads on the florist foam.
4. Add bits of metallic gold filler with wire pins to finish. ✍

Dried Fruit Garland & Ornaments

You can make fragrant garlands and ornaments with dried fruits and spices. Use them to decorate a room or hang them on your Christmas tree.

For the garland: Simply thread dried citrus slices, dried apple slices, dried bay leaves, dried cranberries and cinnamon sticks on a strong buttonhole thread, much like you do when you make popcorn or cranberry garlands. Use a large-eye needle and, before stringing, wax the thread for added strength by running it over a piece of beeswax.

For the ornament: Thread on a few pieces of the dried material on waxed thread, tie the thread, top with a bow, and hang from the tree. ✍

Memory Ornament

This is a beautiful way to celebrate a new baby or remember a loved one, an anniversary, or a special event.

You Will Need:

A clear plastic heart or ball ornament, the type that has two pieces that fit together and opens up

A silica dried flower to commemorate the occasion—a flower that was blooming the day the baby was born (in winter, buy a flower on the baby's birthday from a florist and dry it) or a flower from a wedding bouquet or a special flower arrangement

Other small bits of plant material and/or memorabilia

White craft glue

Ribbon for a bow

Gold cord for hanger

Here's How:

1. Open the ornament. Arrange the flower and the other dried material inside one side of the ornament, using craft glue to secure the arrangement as needed. Make the arrangement large enough so when the other side is attached the flowers will be held firmly in place. Let glue dry completely. To be sure, leave the ornament open for a few days. If any moisture is trapped in the ornament, the flowers will quickly turn brown.
2. Attach the other side of the ornament.
3. Glue the sides together so they are permanently sealed.
4. Add a pretty bow and a gold cord hanger for your ornament. ∾

Dried Rose Arrangement

What could be more lovely than a simple arrangement of dried roses? Add a filler, a beautiful ribbon, and an ornament (here, a butterfly with verdigris finish). ∾

Rose Pomander Ball

Dried rosebuds with short stems make a beautiful pomander. Use a plastic foam ball (such as a Styrofoam® ball) for a base. Glue moss on the ball to cover it, using white craft glue. When the glue has dried, press the stems of the rosebuds in the ball. Add a cord or ribbon for hanging. ∾

A dried rose pomander.

Gilded Leaves

This simple gilding technique makes gorgeous golden leaves. Use them strewn on tables, as decorative accents for packages and potpourri, and in dried flower arrangements.

You Will Need:
Glycerin-treated leaves or sturdy dried
   leaves such as bay (see the
   "Preserving the Harvest" section)
Gold, copper, or variegated gold leaf
   (available in fine art supply stores)
Spray adhesive
Freezer paper
Dry paint brush
Straight pins

Here's How:
1. Protect your work surface with freezer paper.
2. Spray a thin coat of adhesive on the front sides (tops) of the leaves. (Pinning the leaves to the freezer paper will keep them from blowing away with the force of the spray.)
3. Lay out a few sheets of metal leaf. Press the tacky side of the leaf on the metal leaf and rub the back of the leaf gently.
4. Carefully tear the gilded leaf away from the sheet of metal leaf. Run a dry brush over the leaf edges to remove excess flakes. ∽

Pressing the leaves, adhesive side down, on a sheet of metal leaf.

Brushing the gilded leaf with a dry brush.

TWIG & VINE PROJECTS

Twigs and vines can be found anywhere in your yard and garden. These are good projects for the whole family.

Twig or Bark Candle Holder

This method of making a pillar candle holder works equally well with pieces of bark, twigs, cinnamon sticks, or even bits of driftwood.

You Will Need:

2 rounds of wood of equal size and shape (You can saw the rounds from a large branch or purchase round wooden plaques from a craft store. The rounds should be about 4" in diameter to accommodate large pillar candles.)

Strips of bark or twigs ranging in length 6-10"

Glue gun and glue sticks

Decorations—dried flowers, pine cones, tiny birds, whole spices, or seashells

A pillar candle

Here's How:

1. Place one of the rounds flat on a level surface. Using a glue gun, adhere the bark or twigs along about half of the edge of the round.
2. Glue in the other round about 6" from the first round.
3. Continue gluing bark or twigs around until the rounds are covered.
4. Decorate the base by gluing on dried flowers, pine cones, tiny birds, whole spices, or sea shells.
5. Place the candle on the top round. ∾

Woodland Twig Basket

This basket was made using old barn wood for the base and fresh alderwood branches and grapevine for the handle. The fresh branches were nailed to the sides and brought over and nailed down on the other sides. After the handle dried, I decorated it with wired cones (see the "Preserving the Harvest" section), moss, and dried pods. This technique also can be used to add twig handles to woven baskets. ∾

Vine Wreaths

If you are lucky to have an abundance of vines available to you, you may consider making your own wreaths. Grape vine, honeysuckle, hops, and willow saplings can all be used to make wreaths.

You Will Need:
Vines
Garden shears

Here's How:
1. Harvest the vines after the leaves have fallen off for the winter. Strip off any remaining leaves left on the vine before proceeding.
2. Take a piece of vine and form a circle that is the size and shape of the wreath you wish to form. Weave the rest of the vine over and around the circle to create the shape.
3. Add additional vines, weaving them in and out of the wreath, always going in the same direction. Keep adding vines until you have made a wreath as thick as you want. Trim ends that stick out with a pair of garden shears.
4. Hang the wreath in a cool, dry area to dry. ∾

Pictured right: *Above, wrapping a vine wreath. Below, a vine wreath after drying.*

94

Twig Frames

For a woodsy, natural look, glue or nail twigs on purchased wooden frames. Decorate the frames with moss, glycerin-treated leaves, or leaves formed out of polymer clay. The large distressed wood frame features a snail formed out of polymer clay and a real shell as accents. ∾

Twig Easel

Twig easels can be made to fit any frame. They take a little patience to create, but you are rewarded with a rustic, practical holder for framed art and photos. The easels are surprisingly strong when finished.

You Will Need:
A selection of dried twigs
Sharp pruning shears
Craft knife
White craft glue or wood glue
Tiny finishing nails
Hammer

Here's How:
To make your first easel, use the illustration as a guide and cut the twigs to the lengths specified. When you have mastered the technique, *you'll be able to create easels of any size to fit your frames.*

1. Using shears, cut three twigs in each length: 9", 1", and 3-1/2". Use a craft knife to neatly whittle the ends.
2. Form the front frame of the easel by nailing the top points of two 9" twigs together with a small nail. (Fig. 1)
3. Nail two 1" support pieces where the frame will rest. (Fig. 1)
4. Glue one 3-1/2" piece as a cross bar, letting it rest on the two support pieces. Let dry.
5. Nail the remaining 1" piece 3" from the bottom of the remaining 9" piece. (Fig. 2)
6. Nail the third leg (the remaining 9" piece) of the easel to the top. (Fig. 3) Carefully arrange the easel at an angle that will hold the frame securely.
7. Glue two 3-1/2" pieces to hold the legs. Let these pieces rest on the front cross piece and the back cross piece. (Fig. 3)
8. Place glue at every joint and at the top. Let dry completely. ∾

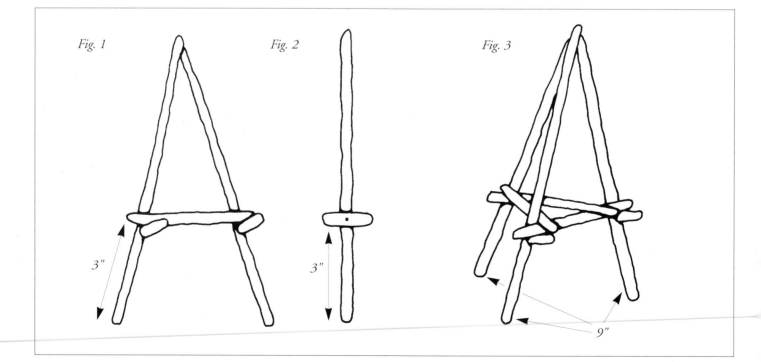

Fig. 1   Fig. 2   Fig. 3   3"   3"   9"

PACKAGING
LIKE A PRO

When you take the time to create beautiful fragrance and culinary gifts, presenting them in an attractive and fun way is equally important. One of the best packaging hints I can give you is to choose a theme for your gift presentation, such as a special occasion, a holiday, or even a color. Using the intended recipient's favorite hobby or sport is another way to create a unique, personalized package. A collection of different theme baskets is presented in the Gift Collections section to inspire you.

Tips for Putting It All Together:

• *Choose a container that fits the theme. It's especially nice when the container is a gift in itself—a flower decorated basket, a dish, or a flower pot, for example— that can be used again.*

• *To display your products attractively, fill the container with a packing material that will hold the products in place and keep them from sliding down. Examples of decorative fillers are excelsior, shredded paper, and tissue paper. If the container is large or deep, pack it with crumpled newspaper first, then place the decorative filler on top. Arrange your wrapped and packaged products on the filler attractively.*

• *To hold everything together, wrap with cellophane or heavy plastic wrap.*

Wrapping Techniques

▓ Wrapping with Cellophane

I prefer crisp, clear cellophane for packaging fragrance and culinary products. Cellophane allows the products to breathe while protecting them from moisture.

Here's How:

1. Cut two pieces of cellophane, each four times as long as the container is high. For example, if your container with the products measures 10" high, cut two pieces of cellophane, each 40" long, from a 24" wide roll.
2. Place the cellophane pieces in a cross formation with the container in the middle.
3. Bring up the ends of the cellophane, two at a time, and gather in your hands. Secure with a twist tie. Trim the ends of the cellophane. Add a bow and a gift tag. ∾

▓ Wrapping with Plastic Wrap

Plastic wrap is especially effective if you are mailing the gift because it helps hold the contents securely. Use heavy plastic wrap for best results.

Here's How:

1. Wrap the collection with plastic wrap, pulling the ends of the wrap to the bottom of the container. Secure with tape.
2. You can further "shrink" the wrap and remove wrinkles by heating with a blow dryer. ∾

Tarragon
Shallot
Vinegar

Bottled Especially
for you by the
Brownings

Beauty Scrub
Facial

Place 1/4 cup of the blend into the
cotton scrub bag. Tie tightly. Wet the
bag well, then rub over your face or
body with a circular scrubbing action.
Discard the contents after use. Rinse
the bag with warm water and lay flat to
dry and use again.

Herbs Aromatiques

Recline and Relax
Bath Herb Blend

Backberry
Brandy

Seasons
Greetings

Citrus
Mint
Window
Spray

Tarragon
Shallot
Vinegar

Millefiori
Bath
Oil

Strawberry
Butter

99

Beautiful Bagging

Bags are wonderful packages for all kinds of gifts—potpourris, herb blends, and mixes for biscuits and muffins, to name but a few. You can buy paper and cellophane bags or make your own bags from laminated decorative paper.

PATTERN FOR GIFT BAG WITH SELF-CLOSING TABS

Pattern is 50% actual size.

Cut along solid lines. Emboss along broken lines.

Tab

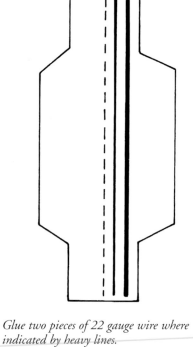

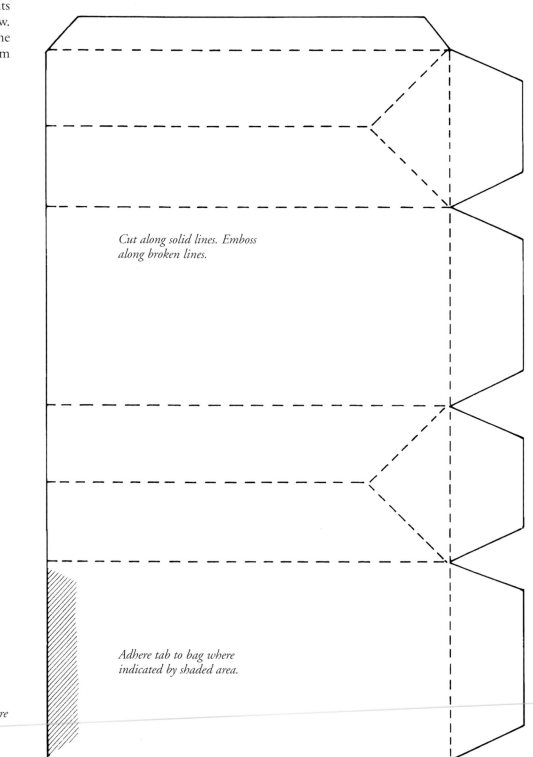

Adhere tab to bag where indicated by shaded area.

Glue two pieces of 22 gauge wire where indicated by heavy lines.

Making Laminated Paper Bags

You Will Need:

Plastic coated freezer paper
Gift wrap paper
Iron and ironing board
22 gauge wire
White craft glue

1. Place a piece of plastic coated freezer paper, shiny side up, on the ironing board.
2. Cut a piece of gift wrap the same size as the freezer paper. Place the gift wrap, with the right side up and the wrong side against the shiny side of the freezer paper.
3. Press papers with a with a medium hot iron to laminate. Let cool.
4. Trace the bag pattern on the blank side of the laminated paper. Cut out, emboss on dotted lines, fold, and glue.
5. Make self-closing tabs for your bags by tracing and cutting out the tab pattern. Glue wire as indicated. Let dry.
6. Glue the tab to the top of the bag. ∽

Sealing Bottles

It is important to properly seal your bottles so the contents won't leak out and spoil. Using sealing wax made for bottles is best—the sealing wax contains a rubber compound which makes the wax act more like plastic than wax, and the seal is leak-proof and attractive. Dipping twice seals the bottle. Many colors are available.

Don't use paraffin or beeswax to seal bottles—the seals eventually will leak, and oils eat right through them.

Basic Method

You Will Need:
Sealing wax
Double boiler
Bottle with cork
Cord or ribbon

Here's How:
1. Place sealing wax in a shallow foil container. Place the foil container in a saucepan or skillet of water to make a double boiler. The wax will melt at 300 degrees F. Watch that the water does not boil over the sides of the foil container into the wax.
2. Fill the bottle you wish to seal and insert the cork snugly, leaving enough cork above the top of the bottle to grasp for removal.
3. Wrap cord or ribbon around the neck of the bottle. Twist at the back and keep taut (Fig. 1), then drape over the top of the bottle, tape in place to hold (Fig. 2).
4. Invert the bottle and dip into the melted sealing wax, submerging the neck of the bottle about 1/2" from the top until an adequate seal has been made. Lift the bottle straight up, letting the excess wax drip away. Let cool and harden.

Decorative Wax Seals

Use inexpensive rubber stamps and melted sealing wax to make decorative wax seals for decorating packages. The process does not damage the rubber stamp, so it still can be used for stamping.

You Will Need:
Sealing wax
A double boiler
Spoon
Aluminum foil
Rubber stamp
White craft glue
Optional: Metallic highlighter cream or wax

Here's How:
1. Melt the sealing wax in a double boiler.
2. Using a kitchen spoon, spoon out a pool of wax about the size of a quarter on a piece of aluminum foil.
3. Immediately press a rubber stamp into the wax. Wait a few seconds before removing the stamp to allow the wax to harden.
4. Let the wax cool completely, then peel away from the foil. If you are not pleased with the result, re-melt and try again.
5. *Option:* Rub the wax seal with metallic highlighter cream to accent.
6. Use thick craft glue to adhere the seals to bottles, packages, and envelopes.

Polymer Clay Seals

You also can make seals with polymer clay. Roll a small amount of the clay into a small ball. Flatten slightly. Push a rubber stamp into the clay to create a decorative impression. Follow the manufacture's directions on baking the clay in your home oven. ∞

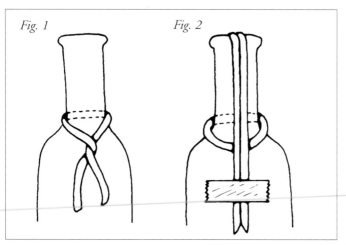

Fig. 1   Fig. 2

Decorative Corks

A decorated cork can be the crowning glory to your gift. Corks can be decorated with beads strung on wire, wooden rounds, or anchored accents.

- **Beaded Wire Cork:** Beautiful colorful beads threaded on wire make distinctive decorations for corks. Make a hole with an awl in top of the cork. Thread colorful beads on a piece of 19 gauge black wire. Curl the top of the wire to hold the beads securely. Dip the other end of the wire into white craft glue, then press the wire into the top of the cork.

- **Corks with Wooden Rounds:** Round thin wooden pieces can be found at stores that sell supplies for decorative painting. They can be painted with acrylic craft paints and decoupaged with photocopies of pressed flowers or accented with charms. Glue the decorated wooden rounds to the tops of corks.

- **Corks with Anchored Accents:** Don't just glue objects such as shells, large beads, or charms to the tops of corks— when you pull on the cork, the object will come right off. Rather, reinforce the object with an anchor. First, take a small screw and screw it into the cork, leaving 1/4" sticking out. (This is the anchor.) Choose an object that fits over this anchor. (Some flat bottomed objects won't work.) Glue the object to the cork over the anchor with a generous amount of thick craft glue. Let the glue dry before using. ∞

HOT
PEPPER
OIL

Making Labels for Your Gifts

It's important to properly label your fragrance and culinary creations. A label should clearly state instructions for use, the "best before" date, and storage instructions.

Making labels is a satisfying finishing step for your wrapped and packaged products. The label should accent the overall package design without overpowering the item. Use hand written labels for a homemade look or create them with a photocopier or computer printer for a more professional appearance. Look in bookstores and art supply stores for books with images designed for copying—buying the book gives you the right to reproduce the images. (**Don't use** copyrighted images.) Select decorative papers for labels and cut the edges with paper scissors specially made for creating decorative edges.

You will find many examples of labels in the "Gift Collections" section, including samples of labels you can reproduce on a copier with your choice of decorative papers. Objects such as glycerin treated leaves, buttons, or wooden clothespins also can be used for labels.

Leaf Labels

Using a gold paint pen, write across glycerin treated or pressed leaves to make a decorative label, place tag, or package tag. ✎

Tarragon Shallot

Dill Lemon Dill

Rose Bowl
Potpourri

Romantic
Bath Herb Blend

Oregano
Oil

FLAVOURED TEA

Beauty Scrub
Facial

Place 1/4 cup of the blend into the
cotton scrub bag. Tie tightly. Wet the
bag well, then rub over your face or
body with a circular scrubbing action.
Discard the contents after use. Rinse
the bag with warm water and lay flat to
dry and use again.

FAIRY
WATER

Making Labels for Your Gifts

▓ Stenciled Labels and Tags

The huge variety of pre-cut stencils available at craft stores makes it easy to decorate labels and tags; you also can make your own stencils for a truly custom look.

When making paper labels, I prefer to use a paper paint or an inked rubber stamp pad, but acrylic craft paints, stencil paints, and stencil gels are also suitable. Use a good quality stencil brush—one with closely packed bristles that feels comfortable in your hand—for best results.

To Cut Your Own Stencil You Will Need:

Mylar® - It is a thin, clear flexible plastic material. Use thin Mylar® for easier cutting. You also can use freezer paper for cutting out your stencil; it is easier for a beginner to cut but it will not last for many repeats. You also can buy stencil blank material in sheets at stores that sell crafts supplies.

Craft knife with a #11 blade

Cutting surface - Use a self-healing craft mat or a piece of 1/4" thick glass with polished edges

Pattern - You can use almost anything for your pattern, as long as it is not copyrighted. Bookstores and craft stores sell a selection of pattern books. Always photocopy the design to make the pattern because you'll cut up the pattern as you cut your stencil.

Tape

Here's How:

1. Tape the pattern you wish to cut to the back of your chosen stencil material.
2. Place the pattern and stencil material on your cutting surface. Carefully cut out the pattern, keeping the blade at a low angle to the surface for best results. Make the cuts clean. Don't over-cut at the ends of the motifs—that will weaken your stencil.
3. Carefully remove the pattern. You are ready to stencil your project. ∽

Adding a stenciled design to a computer-printed label.

STENCIL PATTERNS FOR MEDITERRANEAN BASKET

MEDITERRANEAN BASKET

This gift basket has a bright Mediterranean color scheme and uses classical motifs as accents. The culinary product selection is perfect for a single person or a couple who enjoys entertaining.

The Contents

- Italian Vinegar (see "Culinary Crafting" section)
- Rosemary Oil and Balsamic Vinegar Dipping sauce (see "Culinary Crafting" section)
- Cheese in Oregano Oil (see "Culinary Crafting" section)
- Herb Biscuit Mix (see "Culinary Crafting" section)

Packaging

- The collection is presented on wooden bread board with stenciled edges. The board has been finished with food-safe beeswax polish to protect the surface.
- The labels have been printed on a computer and stenciled with a wreath design.
- The cotton bag holding the biscuit mix and the herb pots also are stenciled.

Nice Additions

- Stenciled terra cotta pots planted with fresh herbs. ✑

Italian
Vinegar

Oregano
Oil

DIPPING
SAUCE
ROSEMARY OIL
BALSAMIC VINEGAR

Mediterranean Blend

NORTH WOODS BASKET

Twig projects, pine cones, and warm spices in rich tones of brown, maroon, and forest green make this a charming culinary gift collection. It's the perfect hostess gift when visiting someone's cabin in the woods.

The Contents

- A selection of herb blends (see "Culinary Crafting" section)
- Garden Herb Biscuit Mix (see "Culinary Crafting" section)
- Flavored Butter (see "Culinary Crafting" section)

Packaging

- A barn wood basket with a twig handle is used for the container. (See "Twig & Vine Projects" section.)
- Natural paper and glycerin-treated leaves make woodsy labels. (See "Preserving the Harvest" section.)

Nice Additions

- Twig and bark-inspired gifts include a twig frame on a twig easel and a bark candle holder with a pillar candle. (See "Twig & Vine Projects" section.) ∾

VICTORIAN TEA TIME

Romantic roses, lace, and soft floral colors make this a very special collection.

The Contents

- Layered Scented Sugar (see "Culinary Crafting" section)
- Currant Fruit Syrup (see "Culinary Crafting" section)
- Strawberry Butter (see "Culinary Crafting" section)
- Candied Ginger Scone Mix (see "Culinary Crafting" section)
- Flavored Teas (see "Making Flavored Teas" in the "Culinary Crafting" section)

Packaging

- The container is a shallow terra cotta pot painted with softly draped garlands of roses along the sides to create a romantic look.
- Frosted glass bottles contribute to the soft look. (You can make frosted glass with an etching kit.)

Nice Additions

- Make a simple fly doily by sewing charms to the points of an old piece of linen.
- Small painted pots ∞

Candied Ginger Scones

Strawberry
Butter

Currant
Syrup

SUMMER PICNIC BASKET

Make a summer picnic a special occasion with this delightful collection presented in a traditional basket that can be used again and again.

The Contents

- Herb Blends for creating favorite dips (see "Culinary Crafting" section)
- Fruit Syrups for making drinks (see "Culinary Crafting" section)
- Strawberry or Raspberry Butter (see "Culinary Crafting" section)
- Pecan Cranberry Muffin Mix (see "Culinary Crafting" section)

Packaging

- The container is a whitewashed picnic basket. The hinged wooden top is covered with fabric. Lace is glued along the edges.

Nice Additions

- Tablecloth and matching napkins with berry napkin rings. (Make each napkin ring by stringing six artificial berries on wire and securing the ends.)
- Beehive tablecloth weights hold down the corners of the cloth in a breeze. The painted wooden beehives have screw eyes in the tops. The clips for attaching them to the corners of the tablecloth can be found at hardware stores in the electrical supplies department. ∽

Strawberry Butter

Blueberry Syrup

Aromatique

Dill

PECAN CRANBERRY
MUFFIN MIX

Pour the package into a large bowl. Add TWO EGGS,
lightly beaten and 1 CUP MILK. Stir until mixture is
just moistened. Fill paper-lined or greased muffin cups
2/3 full. Bake in a 400 degree F oven for 20-25
minutes or until muffin test done.

MILLEFIORI BATH COLLECTION

Millefiori means "a thousand flowers," and this basket celebrates their many colors, shapes, and sizes. This personal fragrance collection features a variety of floral scents.

The Contents

- Botanical Bath Oil (see "Personal Fragrance Crafting" section)
- Millefiori Potpourri (see "Home Fragrance Crafting" section)
- Bath Herbs (see "Personal Fragrance Crafting" section)

Packaging

- Pressed flowers decorate the painted terra cotta saucer and soap dish. (See "Pressed Flower Pretties" section.)
- The bath herbs are presented in handmade bags accented with photocopies of pressed flowers. (See "Pressed Flower Pretties" section.)

Nice Additions

- Wax sachet balls (see "Home Fragrance Crafting" section)
- A pressed flower card (see "Pressed Flower Pretties" section)
- Candle and soap bar decorated with pressed flowers (see "Pressed Flower Pretties" section). ∞

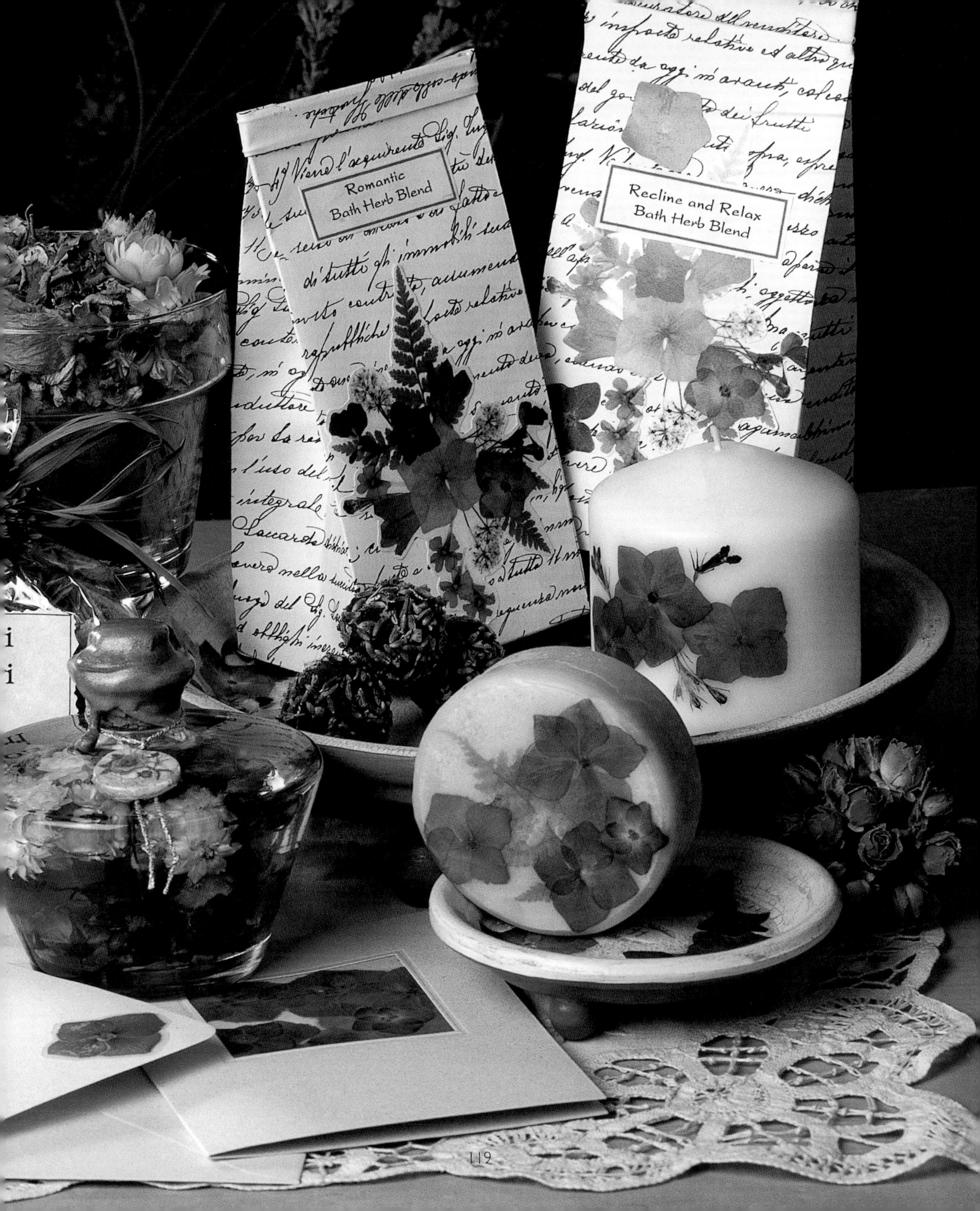
Romantic
Bath Herb Blend
Recline and Relax
Bath Herb Blend

Spring Cleaning Pail

This home fragrance gift basket would make a wonderful housewarming gift. The citrus color theme matches the fresh citrus-mint aromas used to create the products.

The Contents

- Lemon Lace Potpourri (see "Home Fragrance Crafting" section)
- Scented Cleaning Powder (see "Home Fragrance Crafting" section)
- Air Freshener (see "Home Fragrance Crafting" section)
- Lemon Mint Window Spray (see "Home Fragrance Crafting" section)
- Critter Gone Vacuum Sachet Blend (see "Home Fragrance Crafting" section)

Packaging

- Bright metal tins and painted pots with lids hold the cleaning products.
- A large, new galvanized pail holds everything.

Nice Additions

- Rolled up dishcloths in coordinating colors tied with natural raffia
- A citrus colored whisk broom and pot scrubber
- Dried citrus fruits (see "Preserving the Harvest" section) ∞

THE MID...
MANUFACTURED BY
...RN BROO...
...WARE LT...
...R. I

Critter Gone
Sachet

...achet on your rug and leave over...
...the blend in your vacuum...
...f fragrance every time...
...vacuum.

...trus
...int
...adow
...pray

...Cleaning
...wder

...cratching powder fo...
...and counter tops.

Orange
Spice
Air
Freshener

CHRISTMAS WARMTH

This traditional Christmas gift collection is full of natural fragrance products for home and hearth. Every member of the family could help make this basket, starting a family tradition.

The Contents

- Yuletide Star Potpourri (see "Home Fragrance Crafting" section)
- Christmas Tree Simmering Potpourri (see "Home Fragrance Crafting" section)
- Fire Starter Cones (see "Home Fragrance Crafting" section)

Packaging

- Crisp cellophane bags hold fragrant botanical potpourris.
- Label with hand lettered tags and glycerin-treated leaves (see "Preserving the Harvest" section.)
- Accent the packages with rusty tin ornaments.

Nice Additions

- Balloon Shell Candle (see "Pressed Flower Pretties" section)
- Fragrant Citrus-Spice Garland (see "Dried Flower Decorations" section) ∽

Yuletide
Star
Potpourri

Christmas Tree
Simmering
Potpourri

Seasons
Greetings

DELLA ROBBIA BASKET

Luca della Robbia was a Italian designer who lived in Florence in the 15th century. He created terra cotta ornaments for churches that included borders and arrangements of richly colored flowers and whole fruits. This elegant gift collection features rich culinary treats and colors associated with the work of della Robbia.

The Contents

- Tapestry Potpourri (see "Home Fragrance Crafting" section)
- Spirited Fruit (see "Culinary Crafting" section)
- Blackberry Brandy (see "Culinary Crafting" section)
- Currant Syrup (see "Culinary Crafting" section)

Packaging

- The products have been packaged in a terra cotta pot decorated with polymer clay and accented with metallic highlighter cream.
- Gilded leaves accent the packages. (See "Dried Flower Decorations" section)

Nice Additions

- A Della Robbia arrangement made with whole dried fruits, roses, and seed pods (see "Dried Flower Decorations" section) ∽

Spirited
Fruit

Currant
Syrup

INDEX

METRIC CONVERSION

INCHES TO MILLIMETERS AND CENTIMETERS

Inches	MM	CM
1/8	3	.3
1/4	6	.6
3/8	10	1.0
1/2	13	1.3
5/8	16	1.6
3/4	19	1.9
7/8	22	2.2
1	25	2.5
1-1/4	32	3.2
1-1/2	38	3.8
1-3/4	44	4.4
2	51	5.1
3	76	7.6
4	102	10.2
5	127	12.7
6	152	15.2
7	178	17.8
8	203	20.3
9	229	22.9
10	254	25.4
11	279	27.9
12	305	30.5

YARDS TO METERS

Yards	Meters
1/8	.11
1/4	.23
3/8	.34
1/2	.46
5/8	.57
3/4	.69
7/8	.80
1	.91
2	1.83
3	2.74
4	3.66
5	4.57
6	5.49
7	6.40
8	7.32
9	8.23
10	9.14